My Dad and Me:

A Journey of Love, Loss and Life

Daxa Manhar Patel

2QT Limited (Publishing)

Reviews

Daxa has quite literally poured her heart out on paper in order to make sense of the uncontrollable emotion that is grief, and to encourage and provide hope to those currently living with it. The book is a mix of conflicting emotions played out over time – the desire to recount positive memories of her father balanced against the all-consuming sense of loss after he was gone. The grief cycle borne out and re-lived on every page.

The short, conversational style is just like she's talking to you – raw, heartfelt... – all the time questioning why has she been affected for so long. The poetry throughout emphasises the anguish and pain and the beautiful photography representing life and renewal. Anyone that has been close to a parent/ sibling/ friend that has experienced loss will be able to relate to this and yet find significant comfort within its pages.

Suzanna Prout
MD of Xenonex Coaching Talent

Daxa bravely shares the story of her love and grief for her inspirational father. Talking of death and loss is so important for the wellbeing of our society and its individuals.

Kerry Jackson
Former Chief Executive
St Gemma's Hospice, Leeds

Second Edition published 2025 by
2QT Limited (Publishing)
United Kingdom

First Edition published 2020

Copyright © Daxa Manhar Patel 2020
The right of Daxa Manhar Patel to be identified as the author of this work has been asserted by her in accordance with theCopyright, Designs and Patents Act 1988

All rights reserved. This book is sold subject to the condition that no part of this book is to be reproduced, in any shape or form. Or by way of trade, stored in a retrieval system or transmitted in any form or by any means, electronic, mechanical, photocopying, recording, be lent, re-sold, hired out or otherwise circulated in any form of binding or cover other than that in which it is published and without a similar condition, including this condition being imposed on the subsequent purchaser, without prior permission of the copyright holder.

Disclaimer

This book is intended to be a helpful guide to those experiencing grief and is not intended to replace any medical advice. The personal experiences recorded in this book do not offer a diagnosis or any treatment for grief or any medical conditions. If you are experiencing grief, any mental health/ emotional difficulties, you should seek advice from your doctor or mental health therapist.

Cover Design by Gerry Andrews
Images: Author's own except those on pages 45, 109,135 (Pixabay) and page 160 (shutterstock.com)

Printed in Great Britain by IngramSparks

A CIP catalogue record for this book is available
from the British Library

ISBN - 978-1-7385640-8-8

Dedication

This book is a tribute to my magnificent father
Manhar Patel to whom I owe so much.
I thank you Dad for inspiring me to be where I am today.
I am because of You.
I love you Dad and always will
x Your grateful daughter, DMP.

Manhar Patel

Acknowledgements

There are so many kind souls including friends and colleagues who have inspired me and supported me along the way. To preserve confidentiality, I will keep this short but those not mentioned by name, you know who you are. I thank you for your support and understanding while I learn to live again.

Those I acknowledge and thank below have helped me bring this book to fruition.

Jackie Oates, Rashree Soni, Gerry Andrews, Leela Parmar and Nalini Thakkar. My awesome soul friends. Thank you for standing by me.

Kamlesh Patel, my amazing and brilliant running Coach, Dr. Angela Rickards, my father's daughterly Doctor and my caring G.P. and Caroline Harvey, my Bereavement Counsellor and friend, for helping me through those dark days.

Catherine Cousins and her team at 2QT Publishing for their guidance, patience and editorial support from start to publication and beyond. It has been a joy working with you though at times you have had to push me when I hit an emotional wall. I am glad you are on my team.

Gerry Andrews for his artistic and beautiful book cover design. When I described what I thought the cover should feel like you understood and did much more than I could have hoped for. Your hand painting of my father's hand in mine is magnificent beyond words. I cannot thank you enough for all that you have done for me.

All the fabulous writers who have inspired me and helped

through their powerful prose.

And finally, my gratitude to God whom I recognise through my father's eyes, for never giving up on me.

Note from author

If you are reading my words, I thank you from the bottom of my heart. I decided to update my book that was originally published in December 2020 because I feel it is important I offer some help and guidance to my readers, many of whom suffered during the terrible Covid-19 pandemic, and I also wanted to update my readers on my journey of grief and transformation since such a lot has happened since my book first came out.

This book is being updated to mark my dad's 107th birthday in April 2025. My love for my darling dad is even deeper, and I am immensely grateful he walks with me in each step I take.

To my amazing readers, thank you for being a part of my journey.

Daxa Manhar Patel
4th February 2025.

Preface

Thank you for turning a page in this book. As I write this I mark my father's 102nd birthday so it is an auspicious day. My journey of writing started as a blog following the death of my father, and my heartache. I revisit this after six years and four months. I see I have written 42,307 words trying to make sense of my grief journey. This book will be published on 30th December 2020 when it will be seven years to the day of my father's passing.

As a bereaved daughter and not as an expert on grief (still) I have only three top tips:

- Celebrate the happy times you had together.
- Be kind to yourself.
- Don't expect to 'recover'.

This book is dedicated to all those daughters and sons who were blessed like me to have the most amazing and inspirational Dad whose passing knocked you sideways.

The pandemic and the bereaved.

As the pandemic unfolded, I remember clearly sitting on my Swiss ball at home in front of the TV watching the then Prime Minister, Boris Johnson, advise us of the lockdown rules. Like so many I was alone and at home, stuck in my own bubble, just going out for a half an hour run and sticking to the lockdown rules. In awe of all the key workers and worried about all those who were stranded at home and in poor health, I remember not being able to sleep thinking of all the people I know personally who lost a loved one, a parent or a grandma. Many died alone in the hospital with no family member by their bedside, some managed to say their goodbyes through the dreaded oxygen mask, and the PPE-covered kindly hospital medic holding an iPhone to connect them to their families, but many, including a close family member of mine, died all alone.

  I know how hard my own grief journey was when I lost my father, and the circumstances he and I went through cannot compare to what the families endured during the pandemic. The pandemic unfolded a cruel side of our lives over which none of us had any control. People were dying untimely deaths, abandoned, or cared for by strangers, while their families stayed at home, worried sick. I cannot imagine the anguish these people went through but my heart was breaking for them, and I so wanted to reach out to those left behind.

  I did, in fact, send copies of my books to those people I

knew who were grieving during the pandemic, but I want to acknowledge the complexities of the grief that the bereaved will have experienced, and though I cannot possibly imagine how tough it has been for them, I want them to know I witnessed their journey from afar, and prayed for them all.

Grief is as personal as our DNA, and only those walking that journey know how painful it is.

To the bereaved who silently had to endure attending funerals with social distance and no hugs from others, I see you and I hear you. To those who so wanted to be with their mams and dads and hold their hands when they took their last breath, I see you and I hear you. To those who crumbled upon getting the news that their relative was a little poorly when they left in an ambulance but deteriorated rapidly, and they had to be induced into a coma, I cannot imagine your pain, but I do see and hear you.

You went through the darkest of tunnels of grief, and you survived the worst, and it is important we acknowledge your journey and offer our support in whatever way we can. One of my friends told me how she, despite her pressured leadership role which entailed looking after her staff and the service users, shielded her mum by bringing her to her flat from the care home, because she knew that her mam who was partially sighted, hard of hearing and in her late eighties would rapidly go down without her daughter being there for her. This friend of mine rose to the challenge like a gallant soldier and did her utmost to care for her mum against all odds, yet the time came when death knocked on the door, then the grief followed. Many bereaved carers post-pandemic will have endured unimaginable emotional pain which will have compounded their grief. The inquest in the UK through the Covid Inquiry has re-opened these old wounds that had barely healed, and politicians who were possibly well-meaning but out of their depth have seemingly got away scott free, but I challenge anyone to say they were not affected emotionally by the human catastrophe that we all witnessed from our TV screens.

I am not an expert on grief and anybody who says one recovers has clearly not had the privilege of losing someone and feeling the full depth of grief, but as someone who did find her way up from the deep valley of grief, I offer my hand in friendship to anyone who wants to talk or needs support. Being a lawyer, I like to make it crystal clear that I am neither a counsellor nor a trained bereavement expert, but I have an insight into what losing someone you love deeply does to your heart and soul, and I am an incredibly good listener. My take on life is that if I cannot be there for others to help ease their pain then what good is this life of mine?

Sending you much love, and peace. Your fellow traveller.

My journey since 2020.

My book is a compilation of my blogs written in real time over a period of six years following the death of my darling Paa, whom I still love very dearly. I have now graduated to having been on earth for eleven years since my father's physical departure, and to those who read my book and to those who are picking my book up for the first time, I want to share with you where I am because like nature, our lives are like the four seasons, and like grief, one endures deep anguish, pain followed by a sense of surrender, then awakening, and discovery of a new path where we still hold on to our loved one we lost and still love so much, and I certainly feel this.

I do not want to ever get over my father's death and I know why I am still here.

If you are feeling the pain of loss, and you wonder will you ever feel you can keep going, well take it from me, you have no idea how strong you really are.

I have been walking on what seemed a road going nowhere to discovering I am fine with that, because if nothing else, I know one thing; I am walking on a road that is taking me home to my father and to God, because there is no doubt in my mind that one day my father and I will be holding hands while going for a long walk with our German Shepherd dogs walking by our sides, Asha at my dad's side and Oscar at mine.

I have become a regular columnist for the Yorkshire Post since I was asked to write about grief following the death of our late Queen, Elizabeth II. As you can imagine, this has been a real honour and an unexpected gift which came out of the ferocious writing I embarked on after losing my paa.

If I am to sum up my journey since my book was published in December 2020 in few words it is this: I have discovered my calling and my passion for life, and I have gone from not wanting to live another day without my dearest and best friend and teacher, my father, to feeling grateful to God for each day I wake up. I am alive like you, and I have a clear purpose, like you to live life to the full.

My dad and God sent me a soulful gift in the form of a German Shepherd, Oscar Patel, in 2021. He arrived in my world only eight weeks old and the journey he and I have been on ever since will be captured in my forthcoming book where I will share the transformation from a journey of love, loss and life to a journey of love, hope and healing. He entered my world as a soul dog who came to give me what I did not know I needed. Watch this space.

Suffice to say, eleven years on, I have discovered my new purpose and my why, and I know how delighted my Paa is to read these words, because I know he is walking with me every step of the way.

My why

I have discovered after many falls and detours, my why is rooted in honouring my dad's legacy through my actions and impact, embodying his love and support to uplift others. It is a legacy of love, compassion, and service, driven by my desire to be the light for others, just as my father was for me.

To my readers, I will leave you with this gift if you are on your journey of walking through the valley of grief.

You will not just survive; one day you will wake up and realise your grief is your superpower, and you will start to thrive.

Further support and a helping hand

Losing my dad opened a new door in my wonderful journey. I have moved into the room of life where I see light and feel the fresh air, new hope, and new possibilities to make an impact, to help. We are sustained by love, hope and breath.

It took me a good few years to recognise that the reason I resorted to being my own grief 'coach' was because I was alone, and I needed my journey to be acknowledged. My father was my only family and losing him was, as he always said, the making of me.

If you want support or just want to have a friendly chat, do reach out to me; it will be my honour to be of help not least because you know more about me than I know about you, but also because I owe it to you, as you have invested your energy in reading my words, to be of service to you in the best way I can. The very fact that you are holding this book means we have shared a journey of tears, love and hope. We are travellers and I wish you nothing but the best in all that you desire.

Love, light and respect to you, and your loved one in heaven.

Your friend, Daxa

To contact me:
https://calendly.com/daxa_patel/coaching-discovery-call
www.daxapatelresilience.com
Daxa M Patel | LinkedIn
Facebook
Daxa M Patel (@daxamanharpatel)

Dear friend,

In the wake of losing my beloved father, I embarked on a journey of resilience and healing, finding solace in writing about my evolving emotions. While I am not a traditional expert, my experiences have taught me profound lessons about love, loss, and the transformative power of grief. This book is a collection of heartfelt blogs that chronicle my path, offering insights into the emotional roller- coaster that often follows the loss of a loved one. Through sharing my story, I hope to provide empathy, guidance, and comfort to those navigating their own journeys. May this book be a beacon of hope and love as you embrace your path to healing.

I wish you hope and much love along the way..

DMP

102 Not Out ...
Happy Birthday Pops :)

April 26, 2020

I did not have any great plans but I did make his favourite dishes of food, some of which I had not cooked in more than three years. I had to ask my nephew's wife, Deepa, for the recipe as I had forgotten! The day was lovely and sunny like today and it was so beautiful, and all I did was to run, read, write, cook and share some fond memories with those I am close to. It was perfect, a day my dad would have enjoyed just as much as I did.

With the lockdown we have all been forced to hit the emergency pause button. It is deeply sad to see so many lose their lives due to the Coronavirus. However, on a slightly lighter note, we have all been given this opportunity to stand back and reconfigure the greater purpose of our being.

The quiet roads, the community spirit and the sense that we are all in this together has in some ways brought a sense of unity amongst humanity. The air is much cleaner and wildlife is happier so we must ask what more can we do to live a more meaningful existence once the lockdown is lifted.

I have had the chance to run daily and do more yoga. I find more peace in this quiet and slow paced existence. This morning I met one of my neighbours walking with her dog and she said, 'Isn't it lovely,' and I said, 'Yes, it most definitely is.' There is no doubt for some being in lockdown must be incredibly hard and very isolating. I volunteer with Silver Line who have joined up with Age UK. The common theme is we need to reach out and we need to connect more. People who are isolated need to feel they are not abandoned and they are not alone. One of the people I support actually said they were frightened of dying and that they had nobody to talk to about how they felt. I probed them to go deeper into what they felt and what this meant to them. I know I am no expert but why are we still shying away from talking about death and how we feel about it? Death, like birth, is part of our human existence we need to talk about it and also, if we can, we ought to celebrate the lives of those lived, including our own lives.

So many people have lost a loved one so unexpectedly due to this virus. Let us, those who have some insight as to what grief is like, reach out to those and tell them that though they may never get over the loss of their loved one, one day they will hopefully find the strength to celebrate their lives together.

A good friend of mine once told me, 'It is better to celebrate the life of a wonderful soul than to celebrate a life lost.'

My father lives on through me and as far as I am concerned he is with me always. To anyone out there who is on this journey, please take comfort. Love and loss are part of our journey. If we feel both, we are incredibly blessed, for we have known the tenderness of love and the jagged edge of grief. Still we rise as we must.

Peace be with you.

DMP

My Daddy's Keeper

I was first just your darling daughter
Then your carer
Your mother
Your cook, cleaner and driver
And so many things
All in one

Then the lack of sleep
Caught up with me
The guilt got to me
I was half home half at work
And belonged nowhere
I just so wanted to be
Your little girl
And I wanted my Daddy back

So I walked away
From being a lawyer
A head of department
To just being
My Daddy's keeper

So glad we had one year and one week together
Without the pressure of work
Just being with you
Holding your hand
Stroking your forehead
Reading to you
Being with you

So glad I was much more
Than my Daddy's keeper
I became your darling daughter again
And you my darling Daddy again

Daxa Manhar Patel

Published in *An anthology of poems and stories by Carers UK*, 2014.

Why This Book...

September 7, 2014

Universal facts of life are love, life and death. Each one of us, if we live long enough, will experience the death of a loved one. I am a reasonably articulate and intelligent human being yet I have never experienced or indeed understood the emotional, physical, psychological impact of losing someone I love the most until now. I have gone through life thinking I understood the pain of those left behind but I was wrong. Exactly thirty-five weeks ago, 251 days to be precise, my ninety-five-year-old father died very peacefully of old age and frailty even though he had cancer. My dad would often talk about how I would feel after his death and I would reply, 'I will be just fine.' I could not have been more wrong.

I was the lucky one. I had an excellent relationship with my dad. He was my best friend, teacher, mother and father all in one. Not a day or hour goes by when I don't think of him or miss him.

The rational mind knows my dad lived a long life (or he had 'a good innings' as many would say) but to me that means nothing. My father was an incredibly intelligent and witty person. He was self- taught and very well read. A living encyclopaedia. I miss his physical, protective, towering, loving presence and his brilliant mind. Each day it is like peeling an onion, I peel one more layer and realise the scale and gravity of my loss.

I have always been in control of my emotions but his passing floored me completely. No, I am not depressed, what I am going through is healthy grief. I realised around week fifteen that I had to give myself permission to grieve for I have such a beautiful relationship and such an amazing father.

So, why write? Selfishly to help me heal but also to help support those who are in the midst of their own personal journey of grief. I specifically wanted to support all those daughters and sons out there grieving the death of their precious father.

Grief is personal. The depth of the pain is reflective of the quality of the relationship between the two people. If you happen to be reading this, and if it helps you in a tiny way, I will be thankful.

I received support from unexpected sources and from some very kind individuals. This book is dedicated to those lovely people and to all those daughters and sons like me.

Growing Up!

September 15, 2014

Since my dear dad passed I have had to deal with a whole host of issues. Practical, legal and of course, emotional. To say I miss my dad is really an understatement. How my life has changed only I know. I miss discussing and consulting things with him. I miss his guidance and most of all I miss his presence.

I never realised that despite being a fairly competent being I was, until he died, my daddy's little girl. Sounds odd because I am professional, a successful lawyer, an independent woman capable of managing a department and capable of dealing with almost anything.

This grief journey has made me question who I am. Each day goes by and I learn something new about me, about my dad and about how unique our relationship was and still is.

I remember thirteen days after Dad died I found myself totally alone in the house and in this world. I became alone the day he died. A wave of emotions came over me; it was as though I was going out of my mind. I was scared I was going crazy. First time in my life I cried like a baby. Just when I needed my dad the most all I was left with was his photo and memories.

I felt, and still do feel, a profound sense of loss so deep. I understood I had a broken heart. Part of me died the day he died. The many roles I was performing as his daughter, carer, his protector, had gone just in one blow.

Death is severe, it is so final yet it is part of life. My life turned 360 degrees totally upside down. Thinking of ways to answer the question 'How are you?' – a question I dreaded – I started by saying, 'I am devastated, I have lost the most important person in my life,' to saying, 'My life is a work in progress!' My answer would vary depending on who was asking.

I started to read up on grief. I read many books and the one that stands out is by C.S. Lewis, **A Grief Observed**. I searched online for validation that I was not going out of my mind. That I was not overacting. I hated it when my loss was seen as insignificant because my dad had lived a good long life. Now I realise letting go and giving myself permission to grieve was the right thing to do but it is still a work in progress.

Today, I bumped into an old acquaintance. In a very well-meaning way he asked how long will it take for me to recover? I have learnt now not to be offended by such questions. I politely replied, 'I will never get over my father's death and I don't want to get over his death.' I said, 'It may take three to five years before I can 'stand up' again!' The honest answer is I really don't know. Just when I feel I am turning a corner I go back to day thirteen.

In this journey I have learnt to recognise the signs and moments when I am moderately coping to when I am hitting really low. I have learnt to always acknowledge that most people don't know what to say or indeed how to say the right thing. They mean well and they are trying their best to comfort you.

I am still learning. I am trying to grow up! The fact is I am an orphan. This reality is hard to accept. Most people think only children who have lost their parents can be called orphans, not so in my book.

As I write this in the middle of the night, yet another sleepless night, I am in the midst of this turbulent grief journey post eight months. Most people look at me and think I am the same as I was before Dad died. Yes, I look intact but inside I am broken to bits. Doing a lot of things simultaneously, growing up and trying to put the broken pieces in some sort of order. I am not sure I can put the pieces back together but try I must for Dad's sake and for mine.

Peace be with you.

DMP

100 Days to the First Anniversary...

September 21, 2014

In exactly 100 days it will be one year since my father's death. It is said that the first year and all first events such as my birthday, Dad's birthday, Father's Day, first Diwali, first death anniversary etc. are horrendous. It is true. The way I have managed some of these events is by doing something special. Something Dad would have approved of. In ways that would make him proud of me. Something that would make him smile…

I have found 2014 hard. I have never cried as much and I've never hurt as much. So far I have been counting the days since his death. I am turning this around. I am dreading the first death anniversary but it will still come and I will go back to square one I am sure. I have no choice but to deal with this day as best as I can.

The best tribute I can pay to this great man I call my dad is by putting the positive aspects of his life into mine.

I have set myself a 100-day challenge. My dad loved walking. He would walk around four miles daily regardless of the weather conditions. He started walking religiously from the age of seventy-six after a massive heart attack, until age ninety-two. He walked briskly more than an hour daily. When on the odd weekend I joined him for a walk I always struggled to keep up with him he was that fast. My dad lived a well-balanced and disciplined lifestyle which I admired greatly but I have begun to appreciate this more now than before.

My first 100-day challenge as a tribute to Dad is to walk

daily for a minimum of thirty minutes. I started yesterday. Consistency is not my forte but this is a challenge.

My second challenge is to sit still in quiet contemplation for twenty minutes daily. I cannot sit still. My mind is always running riot. I don't recall my dad meditating but he did advocate the power of silence. He would say this brought him closer to God and closer to nature. He would say this practice re-energised him to keep going and to face the challenges of life, which I can say he did with a smile on his face.

The last eight and a half months have been very lonely on this grief journey. But I am pleased my nephew Shardul, who lives 7,000 miles away, has joined me on these two challenges. Shardul had a very special bond with my dad and my dad was very fond of him so I am comforted that I am not walking this grief journey totally alone.

For me, if I can do these two things on a daily basis for the next 100 days, it will feel good.

As I end this blog I will leave you with one thought. You don't need to look too far for inspiration. It is closer than you think and if you look hard enough you will find that you inspire others as they do you.

Just before my dad died I found this quote: 'O' God, show me the truth about myself no matter how beautiful it is…' I cannot remember where I found it but I placed these words on the study door and they are still there.

Peace be with you.

DMP

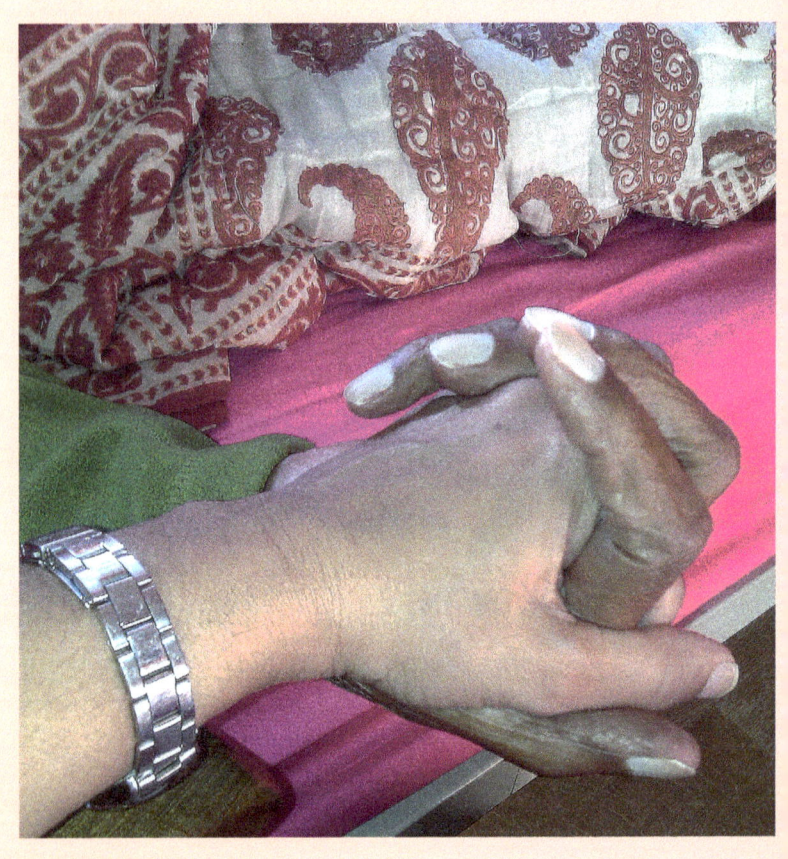

In Life and in Death We are Together

October 2, 2014

It is nine months and I have begun to realise my dad has not left me at all. He is with me. Every step I take, in my highs and lows we are still together.

Until my father died I was oblivious to the impact his physical absence would have on me. In the early days the rawness of my pain sent me into denial. Every single cell of my being was shaken to the core. I had to reinvent my relationship with him. Am I still his daughter or was I his daughter? Is he my dad or was he my dad?

The truth is I cannot bear to live this life of mine without him in the frame. I am because of him. Period.

If I hear comments like, 'You need to move on' I freeze. How and why am I meant to move on? What I have learnt is I will learn to adjust and adapt to life without his physical presence but I have a built-in strength that keeps me going. My dad is with me. When I am driving he sits next to me only I don't see but I feel his presence. When I have some important news to share he is aware. Even God knows it would be a disaster to separate us.

I think we are introduced to God, the creator, the universe through our parents' unconditional love. If the soul is eternal then it follows our relationship does not die with the death of a human being. If we accept that there is such a thing as unconditional love which we cannot see or touch then it follows that love exists in the universe. Love does not die with the death of a human being.

My conclusion therefore, is that in life and death my Paa

and I are together. Knowing this I have the capacity to keep going.

Peace be with you.

DMP

Held

December 28, 2014

Falling
Sinking
Almost drowning
In free fall
Reality
Life has changed
My father's comforting hand
His soothing voice
His smiling eyes
The comfort
The confidence
He gave
Gone for good
As I fall further
I have lived
Survived this first year
Only just but I have
This journey of grief
These dark days of pain
I'm held by God and Pa
The invisible hand
Protecting me
Holding me
He is there
Watching
Listening
I am standing
Amazing Grace
I AM HELD

DMP

The First Year

December 28, 2014

It is almost a year since my dear father passed away. I have not been able to post a blog lately as I just did not have the words to describe my journey.

Survival has been my only aim. I am hanging on, how I have made it thus far even I wonder.

My father was my perfect father. My hero and my anchor. Here I am drifting but hanging on trying to remember all the survival tips he taught me. Like others I too will survive, I just have to. There has to be a reason for this pain and a reason why I am still here.

Nobody and nothing can fill his place in my life. Yes, even at my age I am an orphan. The quote by Antoine Francois Prévost comes to mind which resonates. 'A father is the masterpiece of nature'.

He just gave me unconditional love and care. As he was proud of me I was more proud of him. Even at the age of ninety-five he would enquire how the FTSE was doing! His brilliant mind and the long conversations I so miss.

Some are surprised my tears are still there. Comments like, 'Are you depressed?' or 'You need to snap out of it', and 'You must move on' really are insensitive. Those who have not been here cannot understand.

I still have days when I lose control. I can be walking looking at the sky and without any effort tears flow. I still can't listen to Papa's favourite music or cook his favourite food. Yet the next day I will get up and go. Almost like a robot.

The scale of the devastation in my life only I know yet I

look fine to others. I am comfortable and, yes, I am working so all is normal. But it is not. Part of me died the day my father died. I feel like I have to climb Mount Kilimanjaro and I am still at base camp or like a child learning to walk again. Falling yet trying to get up.

The thing about grief is that when you have least energy you have to make every effort to dig deep to find the energy to keep going.

I am fatherless, I am a bereaved carer and I am an orphan. I don't want sympathy; I am a daughter who has a right to grieve the death of her father. Other daughters may not feel like I do. They were not as lucky as I.

I cannot say I was looking forward to December but it came anyway. The Christmas tree was decorated as my father would like. Cards were sent. The show carries on.

I am not eagerly awaiting the first anniversary or indeed the New Year but it will still come.

I so wanted to put a positive spin on all this sadness and I had to do something meaningful to mark my father's first year of freedom from planet Earth. Christmas hampers were distributed to our local senior citizens who are housebound and over the age of ninety. I think Dad would have approved.

I have no fixed plan for the actual day. I will just go with the flow. He is with me always and forever. That is the only thing I do know.

I will leave with a few lessons of life my father taught me, so here goes…

1. Give money to those in need. At least 10 per cent of one's income should go to worthy causes. As charity begins at home, donate locally first.
2. Always know where you will be in ten years' time and

    never compromise on your principles.
3. Understand and appreciate three things: money, the economy and human psyche.
4. Love is the only thing that matters, the rest will follow.
5. Be happy, God has given us everything we need.

To those reading this post, if you are going through your own journey of loss let it be. It is okay to grieve, it is normal. The deeper your love the more it hurts but that is good, you are blessed to have had such a beautiful relationship which nobody can take away from you.

Peace be with you.

DMP

The Reality of Death

March 12, 2015

As I make sense of the pain of separation caused by my father's death I cannot help but be surprised by how blessed I feel to have had such a magnificent relationship with my only parent. My parents separated when I was young and I was raised by my dad.

Grief is, and can be, a healthy 'normal' response to the death of someone you love and in my case someone significant whom I loved and admired the most. It is okay to feel sad just as it is okay to feel peace when you recall happy memories.

Fourteen months on, what has worked for me is just letting go. I went from being someone totally in control (well I wrongly presumed I had control) to being someone who had no choice but to let go. I had never experienced the torrential waves of grief, consequently I was totally unprepared for the aftermath.

To put it mildly I was shocked as to how low and despondent I felt. Letting go and allowing myself to have good and not so good days meant I was accepting that what I was going through was necessary to embrace this life-changing event.

Certain harsh realities came to the surface and will no doubt continue to unfold as I walk forward.

The death of my dad means there is nobody on this planet (save for the Almighty) who will love me unconditionally the way my father did. There is nobody who knows me better than my dad. He was always my next of kin right until the end. I was the apple of his eye. I won't be that for anyone else, ever.

There is no father here who will be delighted when I am happy or when I reach my personal goals or success. I miss the unspoken words of understanding and comfort he relentlessly gave me all my life. He was always there to love me, if only I understood then what I know now.

I am not saying this to evoke sympathy or pity. It is my reality which I must come to terms with. My father means so much more to me than I ever cared to appreciate while he was alive.

However, death does not end our emotional bond as I am still my father's daughter. I am not done being his daughter. As I continue to unravel this mysterious journey mixed with pride and pain I hope I can be of support, no matter how small, to those facing the realities of death. Often, a griever just wants someone to listen to them without judgement, and that's all.

Peace be with you.

DMP

15 Months On...

April 9, 2015

I am told the passage of time helps. I am not sure of that yet. I do have good days when I feel I can continue to live without my father's physical presence and then just when I kid myself all is well I slip down the deep valley of sadness.

When I have a bad day I really feel surprised, shocked even and numb. In the next few days I will be celebrating my father's 97th birthday. My dad had the zest for life. He wanted to reach 100.

We, as in my dad and I, were lucky that we had as long a spell together, many are not that fortunate. I also know how blessed I am that I was able to enjoy his intellectual company right until the end.

The other day I walked past the greetings cards section in our local supermarket. I will still buy a card for his birthday but this does not take away the blunt awareness of his physical absence.

Half the time I just cannot articulate how raw I still feel. I rejoined my old law firm recently. Going back there has been really nice for I am with friends, but a small part of me has been reacquainted with the deep grief I felt in the early days. I am meeting friends who were with me on my journey when I was my dad's carer. During the day I have panic attacks and I feel like I am going backwards to the day he died. I am reliving the pain of losing him as friends come to see me to express their condolences. It's a double-edged sword. Touched that people care and dread that I may not move forward.

A lot has changed in my life on all fronts yet I still wish I had his presence. Going home to an empty house and seeing his still empty chair is a solid reminder of the finality of death.

Not being able to discuss what I did at work with him and worse still not being able to hear his voice. All the little things I took for granted I now appreciate with a degree of guilt. Just wished I had appreciated him more in life than now.

Fifteen months on, yes, I have moved a step or two but my heart is very much broken. Like a broken expensive vase that cannot be put together ever again.

I am trying to put a brave face on and I can get through the day-to-day practicalities of life. What I am still searching for is my mojo and a reason to live.

I hope one day I will find this. For now I will end this post on a positive note. I am celebrating my father's 97th birthday with a few friends at home hopefully, if the weather is lovely and sunny, just like my dad loved. I will mark this day outside in the garden with good company, tea and his favourite food.

If you are on a similar journey hang in there.

Peace be with you.

DMP

17 Months and 1 Week

June 7, 2015

How long does it take to come to terms with my father's death? Some are surprised that I am still missing my dad. I have heard time is a healer and it won't go away. From experience I think it is the latter. I will never be the person I was before his death. My father's death has left a big hole in my heart. There is risk of sounding melodramatic but honestly I feel there is a deep wound which is still bleeding.

I don't want to ever get over my father's death. He was such an important part of my life and he still is. I have recently come back from a holiday of a lifetime yet I still feel joyless and empty. This month I will have to endure my second Father's Day without him. Truth is, no amount of money or luxury can fill the void left by my dad.

Sometimes I hurt so much that without any effort tears flow. I can't help it and frankly I don't care what others think. It is easy to pass judgement and to offer advice when others have no clue as to what you might be feeling. My father died seventeen months and one week ago but it feels like yesterday when my world fell apart.

I am working and doing all the practical things yet I feel I am barely surviving. Looking at breathtaking scenery on the cruise to Alaska reminded me of the missed opportunity. I could have, and should have, taken my dad on a holiday like this when he was fit and healthy. The guilt and regret I must live with.

I shared the happiest moments of my life with my dad. I often wonder, will I ever feel pure joy and happiness? Will I ever be free from the profound sadness which has been my constant companion for the last seventeen months?

  I tell myself, I am God's child too and I deserve to be happy but the person who gave me life has gone and with him the light inside me has gone out. Despite all this, I live in hope that one day my soul will sing and dance again. This may take many years. I just can't make an educated guess for this thing called grief.

Peace be with you.

DMP

600 Days...

August 24, 2015

As I mark 600 days today since my father's death, I reflect on what I have learnt in the hope that my journey will offer some hope to a daughter or a son in the midst of their deep grief.

This journey is not easy and, no, it does not get easier either. I still miss my dad like crazy just like I did when I first realised after his funeral that his passing had changed my life forever.

The difference between then and now is that I am almost my own expert. I can spot events, places and scenarios that have the potential to lift my spirits or take me down. I am not quite there yet as I am taken aback very surprisingly just when I tell myself I am doing okay, but I know now when that happens, just let it be.

Grief is not a predictable journey. Some experts have commented on the shock, anger, denial, numbness and adjustment phases which I can relate to but my grief is unique to me. It is as unique as our DNA, unique to my closeness with my father and it is unique to our relationship so there is no comparison to be had.

I will say by all means read what others have to say but use what works for you and discard the rest.

This is what I have observed and learnt from my grief journey 600 days on:

1. It is true it is hard for others to understand me or my grief. Why should they? They have not walked my journey and how can anybody understand how

special my dad was to me? Why should they get what my pain or sadness is about? That said, I have come across some genuine friends and complete strangers who don't pretend to understand and that is often a starting point.

2. Don't fight tears – I've never cried myself to sleep nor have I shed so many tears as I have in the last 600 days. Those few who have seen me cry have never seen me cry before. At first I would apologise but I don't anymore. It is really okay. Five months into my grief I realised I had no control. The feeling of grief and deep sadness was so numbing and profound that I surrendered to it completely. I gave myself permission to grieve; after all I had lost the longest relationship I had had since I was born. The one person I trusted the most was gone, how was I was supposed to be? I knew I had to grieve so that one day I could stand up and walk again. My current description of my grief is like making an emergency stop after driving in fifth gear. I hear a loud bang, it transpires it is an earthquake and I am in the midst of heavy fog with no visibility when I lose dad but then slowly I can see the road ahead. There is debris around me, the road is cracked, some buildings have crumbled but there are some intact. I am driving in second gear hanging on to what's left of my life and things that are familiar, knowing full well that my home may not be there but I still need to find my way home. Anything that offers you any form of stability even if it is temporary is worth holding on to, such as work. My work has been my saviour.

3. Be kind to me – it really is easy for me to beat myself up but if there is one time in my life I need to lower

my expectations of me or give myself some slack it is now. Nobody can do that, only I can. I have very high standards and expectations of how I should be. I thought I would be just fine when my father died. I was never so wrong. In the depth of my grief I wasn't a professional trying to manage a difficult situation – that would be easy. I was my daddy's little girl totally lost and yearning so that I could hold his hand and he would guide me out of this fog. This is the time I needed his hand on my head the most to tell me everything would be fine but he had to go and I had to face this on my own.

4. I will never get over his death – his death is not like a broken limb. I have a broken heart but I breathe. I look just fine. It would be an insult to both my father and I if I get over his death. I have come to accept that in many ways through me my father lives on. Not a single day has gone by when I have not spoken to my dad. I say 'good morning' and 'good night' just like before. I know he is not here in the physical form but I can't imagine living the rest of my life without my dad being part of my life. 'Moving on' is not the right phrase to use but perhaps 'moving forward' may be!

5. Forgive myself – I can carry regrets of things I did or words I said that caused hurt to my dad but he was so magnanimous he never held that against me. I can't change the past but I can learn from it. My father loved me. Period.

6. Forgive those who unknowingly trespass and cause hurt – I could write a long list of insensitive comments and remarks I have had but it won't help. Remember, most people mean well and so it is best to forgive them.

7. Self-preservation – this can be mistaken for self-indulgence. Do what you feel is comfortable and right for you. Avoid people and places that drain you. I noticed my energy levels are significantly lower than before, I am easily tired and exhausted I don't have the energy to engage in meaningless small talk. I recognise that and give a wide berth to anything or anyone that is likely to upset my balance of mind.
8. Be grateful – I count my blessings. I am grateful to all those kind souls who have dipped in and out of my life to lend me support of some kind. I am grateful to God, for I know more than ever I have been held. I am grateful to myself, for I am dealing with the most difficult phase of my life in a commendable manner. I am grateful to my wonderful father and for our relationship. He made me feel very special and invincible. I thank him for his constant guidance through this maze even though he is not here in person.

If you happen to come across this post because you are going through a difficult journey yourself, don't lose faith. After 600 days of being in my mental and emotional war zone with myself I am still standing. And so will you. Just be patient and take it one moment at a time.

Peace be with you.

DMP

843 Days On ... Do I Miss Him Less?

April 8, 2016

It has been a long while since I have posted a note. This is largely because I felt I was unable to share my thoughts. Having gone past the two year milestone I felt maybe I am overindulging in my grief or worst still, wallowing.

I mentioned this to a friend. I told him I am running out of patience with myself I need to snap out of the sadness zone. I don't need others to put pressure on me, I do it myself.

I did the openly grieving of my loss and then reached a point of where perhaps I was behaving like a 'victim'. We live in a culture of being able to fix everything but certain aspects of life just cannot be fixed, that is something I am beginning to realise and accept.

The hardest part of this journey of losing my dad is that here I am living with this huge void in my life. My father was my rock, inspiration and strength so life without his towering presence is empty, but I am still going about my daily life, going to work, taking care of me and other social commitments, attending to not so important yet necessary chores of routine life.

In between all this I still have moments when I crumble and wonder why I am still here feeling the pain of his absence. Sometimes it is so palpable that it surprises me but I have to give myself credit for continuing to live, pretending that all is well when, in fact, it is like I am eating food without salt. My life purpose and meaning was all intertwined with my dear father, that's how important he was to my existence. Often I feel paralysed, aching to hold his hand wondering if he has eaten and wondering if he needs me to comfort him as that is how our life was towards the end of his journey. I only really cared for him in the last three years of his life but I cannot seem to go past this point, for we had a long life together when it was my father who looked after me.

I am still acutely aware of how many days it is since he passed. I hardly share this with others as I have resigned myself to this fact. Most people, unless they have suffered a significant loss, will not understand and why should they either. I am blessed there are a handful of people in my life who do care and do understand.

I have to still move forward but I will never get over losing him. This month I will mark what would have been my father's 98th birthday. I always made a fuss on his birthday, having a large group of people at our home was the norm. However, for the first time I feel I just want to mark this day by myself. I can't seem to shift this feeling. I owe it to myself as his passing is my loss and mine alone. I have already taken a bold step as I have pledged Dad's mobility scooter and his wheelchair to a charity and these items will be collected on his birthday. I have not yet planned how I will mark this day but I will do something special in a low-key fashion.

Ironically, though my dad is not here in my physical world, I always feel him by my side. I still talk to my dad daily. For almost two years I was not able to paint my fingernails – something I enjoyed doing before – and whenever I did paint my nails I would show them to my father. He would smile and tell me approvingly that I should do what makes me happy. I have started to use nail polish and I still show him my painted nails but to his photograph. He has never left me but it takes time to get used not having him in my physical world, although I am getting there.

Someone said grieving is like a sacred pilgrimage. I would

say it is also a tribute to love. It takes courage and strength to walk this journey but I feel humble and honoured that I was blessed to have such a wonderful father in my life and blessed to have walked the last 843 days. Life is a blessing and it is an honour to feel this raw pain for it is proof of a life well lived. Happy birthday, my dear wonderful Pops.

Peace be with you.

DMP

Happy 98th Birthday My Dear Pappa

April 21, 2016

A kind soul sent this to me…

> *'Behind every great daughter*
> *There is a truly amazing dad'*

All I can say is, yes, my father is perfect, simply the best. I had the privilege of walking to the summit of the highest mountain with my dad and what a fine journey together it was.

I love you Papa and always will.

DMP

Almost 1,000 Days

August 18, 2016

I am on day 959, not long before I reach 1,000 days after becoming an adult orphan and being without my amazing dad.

Still incomprehensible that I have survived his death but I have. Not a long time in the scheme of things compared to the decades I had with my dad.

My father used to say a new business needs 1,000 days to break even. That is not making profit but just getting to the point of breaking even. I use the same analogy with my life. I set myself the challenge of reaching 1,000 days with a sense of being able to cope with life.

I still feel no joy but I am managing much better that's for sure. I have blocked the very dark days from my memory. Occasionally, when I remember those days, I realise how deep my pain was. My sole purpose now is to motivate myself to get through one moment at a time. I still cannot think too far ahead and that suits me.

I have gone from experiencing the raw grief of being lost to knowing I am stronger than I thought I was. So many have made the same journey so I am not unique but my journey is unique to me. My journey of grief and growth is a reflection of the beautiful relationship I still have with my dad.

When I reflect on life since my dad's passing I know I have reached a point of equanimity. I have noticed a small shift inside me. This year I began to pay more attention to my wellbeing. I have embraced my father's hobby of walking daily which has had many benefits. My fitness has improved and so has my mood. Most importantly I am able to cope with the day-to-day challenges.

My primary aim is to please me, that's not being selfish but it is being respectful to myself. I heard you cannot live a brave life without disappointing some people. My invincibility has returned. I care about what I think first.

The journey of grief, though the most difficult phase of my very privileged life, has been a blessing. I have changed a little inside, but I am still a work in progress. I know I am better than I used to be.

I appreciate everyday 'small' things, like the smiling rose in our garden planted by my father, the row of grand old trees on my route to work majestically waiting for me each morning, and a stranger's smile. Life is a divine gift and we are all intended to be here.

At work I believe I have more empathy for my clients, my emotional intelligence is better than before and I am very grateful to every single soul who walked into my life to help me get up from the floor. Some were friends and some were my teachers but every single one of them helped me grow.

When I walked away from my profession to care for my dad I was quietly confident I would be able to pick up where I left off. I am grateful to be back with my 'old' law firm and back to being a Partner again. My firm, work, clients and great colleagues have been a saviour. I cannot emphasis how very important it has been to be busy and to have a structure. To anyone going through this journey I would say if you can cope, resume work of some kind. It helps to help others and it helps to keep busy.

My friends, some new, some old, have walked with me on and off. I will always be grateful to all these kind souls for giving me their time and patience. For seeing me cry and for

listening to me. For sharing some of my highs and lows along the way.

To sum up this journey thus far:

I've wailed, cried, crumbled, struggled and withered. I read and wrote reams of pages. I've analysed and rationalised only to let go with the flow knowing I had no answers other than to just be.

Then I've walked, worked, run and here I am standing tall. Aware and a little enlightened by this journey. I've broken open to allow a crack of light to come through and feed my soul.

I will end this note on what makes my heart sing, which rarely happens. A few days ago I met a gentleman from Toronto, he knew my dad from his university days. I had heard so much about this gentleman from my dad. When I met him for the first time since I was a toddler he said beautiful things about my dad. Most of all he said he saw a bit of my father's determination in me. That was divine to hear. I hope I can live up to being my father's legacy.

To those experiencing the loss of a significant person, I say have faith in yourself and the creator. We have the choice of staying as a caterpillar or aspiring to transform into a butterfly. Hold your nerve and don't give up.

My tips:
- Believe in yourself.
- Let go.
- Set tiny goals.
- Don't give up on you.

Peace be with you.

DMP

1,000 Days

September 26, 2016

Today has arrived. It is exactly 1,000 days since my dear father's death. I have been thinking what to say. To be honest I doubted I would get here, let alone feel the way I do at this stage. I won't beat about the bush, I feel invincible, unbeaten yet humble for breaking so magnificently.

I could list the heartache and depth of despair or I could put a positive slant on an event I cannot undo.

I've grown and have learnt about my inner strength. When you are exhausted and have nothing left you dig deep to find the courage to keep going, that is when you realise there is more to you than what is obvious even to yourself.

Along the way I have met some lovely kind kindred spirits, some new people have come into my life, and some I thought I knew but got to appreciate them even more. They've helped me in ways they may not know.

I have learnt to live and nurture me, my soul, body, emotions, mind and intellect. I have appreciated the little things in life more than before and I am inspired by what I see.

The work I do as a lawyer has been a saving grace. Apart from giving structure and meaning to my working week my 'old' firm, my colleagues and my clients have all helped me reconnect to what I am good at. I feel honoured to have the chance to make a difference to the lives of others.

Since my dad's death I have done many things for me which I most probably would not have done, such as having a tattoo to mark Father's Day; running the Great North Run – my first half marathon; taking control of my health by walking and taking care of myself; going on retreats to lift my soul, and connecting with people who inspire me.

The sense of gratitude I have is more profound. I know I have been held and supported by the universe and God. Yes, I believe there is higher divine source which is taking care of me.

Amidst all the positives I still do miss my dad's voice as well as his calming and dynamic presence yet I know he's not left me. I feel him and know that in every breath I take he is with me willing me on to live and to smile again.

Having reached the 1,000th day is like crossing the finishing line of my 10km run, but I know I probably still have a full marathon to do metaphorically speaking so I am not done yet but I know I can keep living and maybe one day I will thrive with purpose, joy and love. One lives in hope.

What I have learnt from my father is that each day is God's gift. Make it count and make a difference to yourself and those around you.

So, my gift to my father on this 1,000th day is to say, 'Thank you, dear Papa, for letting me be your daughter. I want you to be happy and free. You can let me go and not worry about me. I have the tools and the confidence to move forward and you are going to be with me always.'

To those sons and daughters walking this path, please don't lose faith. Like me, you probably have inherited much more than just being your father's child. I know I have inherited his indomitable spirit and like him I will smile and carry on.

A good friend referred this quote to me: 'I have been through the fire now I will not fade in the sun.' This encapsulates my present state of mind, who knows about tomorrow!

Peace be with you.

DMP

2 Years 11 Months and 3 Weeks...

November 24, 2016

So, here I am about to mark three years of surviving 'alone' after my father's physical death.

Alone is the reality, I don't mean that in a self-pitying way, far from it.

I have been walking on this road constantly alone; that is the reality of anyone and everyone who loses a much-loved one in their life. Losing a parent even as an adult is a 'game changer' for want of a better phrase, you either make it or don't. Even as an adult I am an orphan and that's a fact of life.

I keep reminding myself that I am not unique in that respect but the journey is mine and unique to me. Unique as the love I shared with my dad, unique as the unconditional love he had for me, which is irreplaceable and will always be.

So, what's it like to have walked alone for almost three years? Sometimes I feel, wow I've made it I can't believe I have survived, and sometimes I hit rock bottom. As time goes on the fall to the bottom is harder because I have more good days now, but the tools I have picked up along the way do help to make the climb out of the bottom a little easier. One thing that is constant is despite the smiles, the discipline and the occasional joy (yes, I do feel that too now) there is a deep sadness I cannot shift. I mostly don't give it room to remind me but it is always there.

In the scheme of things three years may sound like a long time but it is not as in my case I spent a lifetime with my father and only a small time without him. In life he was my rock, I still think he is though he is not here. He certainly still inspires me to be my higher and better self. Even when he was frail and closer to death he still had my back, and though I walk tall there is a huge hole, the void is too huge to even describe.

I sometimes say to myself, I'm so proud of how I have conducted myself since losing my dad and I hope he too is proud of me. When I have good news to share I yearn to see his smiling eyes and wish for his hand on my head. I still want to have a conversation with him about, say, Brexit and the US elections! Without words I knew he loved me the most and our communication even in life was often without words as I feel it is now, but what I wouldn't do to hear his voice again.

These lines resonate…

> *'Where you used to be*
> *there is a hole in the world,*
> *which I find myself constantly walking*
> *around in the daytime,*
> *and falling in at night.*
> *I miss you like hell.'*
> **(Edna St. Vincent Millay)**

There is a silver lining to this journey and grief is a roller coaster of emotions, when you have no option you become strong. That's it.

I will end on this note by referring to yet another quote which sometimes conveys my thought as often words are hard.

'Look closely and you will see almost everyone is carrying a bag of cement on their shoulders. That's why it takes courage to get out of bed in the morning and climb into the day.' (Edward Hirsch)

I would say to those on a similar journey don't lose heart as like me, you will get through, just feel grateful to have loved and lost. It is empowering for sure. Believe me, you will get through and you will find the strength to get through.

Finally, this is my saving grace…

> *'A smooth sea never made a skilful sailor.'*
> (Old English Proverb)

Peace be with you.

DMP

Time Moves Slowly

Time moves slowly
Effortlessly
Yet painfully

The sense of joy
Lacking
Missing
Waiting hopefully

The once smiley face
Now hardly smiles
Clutching at straws
I hang on
Live on but why?

The hollowness inside
Rattled by grief
I hope it's brief

I want to go on
To be his legacy
To be his pride
Thank you Lord
For I was loved
And to love

My soul is grateful
Graceful
And respectful

Searching for peace
Lost sense of joy
Live on hopefully

Time moves on
Effortlessly
Yet hopefully.

DMP

The Third Year!

December 16, 2016

Yes this month is a month of retracing our last moments together though I try not to, but the last month is etched in my soul so deep that I recall exactly what Dad and I did on this day three years ago.

Today, three years back, this was to be our final three-hour drive. My father passed away ten days later. I remember he was his usual happy self despite the fact that he had a catheter bag. He loved our long drives and I loved his company.

That day it was just me and my father. Not once did he say he was tired. I wheeled him into the car and off we went for our long drive. We went to the temple and then to a nearby city. The note in my journal confirms it was great, just me and my Paa, the formidable duo that we were. Just the two of us, it was just so perfect. If I asked my father if he was okay he would always reply, 'I am very happy'. By then he was quite frail but there was something inside him so strong which spurred him on. Looking back I am surprised he had the stamina to get up, let alone stand and sit in the wheelchair or car but he did that. He lived for me and he stretched his life longer than was practically possible, just for me.

The timing of my father's departure was right but I still miss him so much. I have got my head round the fact that he is still with me in my thoughts, my mind and in my heart. I don't feel it's three years, it just seems he is still with me. I go home to him. I still talk to him and tell him about my day, about my highs and my lows. The only thing is I have to imagine his response. I don't hear his voice but I hear him in my heart and can always visualise his smile.

I still have not decided how I will mark the third anniversary of his passing but I know I will do something special. Christmas Day and New Year's Day, well I can't think that far ahead. December is not my favourite month!

Peace be with you.

DMP

Almost...

December 29, 2016

As I approach the third anniversary of my father's death, I feel despite everything the ground beneath me disappeared for a while. In fact, this week feels like the hardest and I have yet to get through the day itself. It has been a while since I have felt so melancholy and sad like this, so much so that I am struggling to snap out of it though I know I will. This year so many things have been positively uplifting and I have had more days of feeling I am close to being at peace with my loss. However, the fall is higher when it does happen and that is probably why I feel like this month couldn't end soon enough for me.

I am beginning to realise the depth of my connection with my father. We live through so many changes as not one moment can be the same as the next, yet the one constant love in my life was that of my father since I was born. The light of his presence never flickered, he was always there looking out for me no matter what. He understood my heart and I realise now that what I had with him I will never, ever have with another human being.

My father is irreplaceable, nothing and nobody can fill the big void left in my soul. Not even God.

My father was ninety-five when he passed. He was incredibly independent until the age of ninety-two so I only became his carer for the last two and a half years of his life. What I miss now are all the years he and I had when he was my soul mate, my buddy and my teacher. We were on the same wavelength on many subjects yet we were very different also. That said, if I was the apple of his eye he was my hero, nothing ever came between us that's how strong we were.

I have been thinking how to mark the third anniversary but I have felt out of sorts of late. I have kept myself busy as I knew I would struggle a little this month with it being Christmas then the anniversary, and what follows is the reflection before the New Year comes in.

My energy levels are so depleted I am, as a close friend said, 'running on empty' so I am keeping my head down and keeping things low-key. I have invited my closest friends. Together we will have tea and we will remember the happy times we all had with my father as he had a special bond with each of us.

This journey is a mix of inner growth. I know how much I have learnt about my own strength and resilience and how much I value the beauty I am surrounded by. Yet it can be equally emotionally exhausting. It is so tiring at times that I just go into self-preservation mode. I pull the shutters down and wait until I am ready to face the world again.

To help me through Christmas I kind of had a plan to get by. It is said that when we know we are about to hit turbulence it is helpful to plan the day in advance. On Christmas Day I decided I would spend the day delivering hampers and visiting the over-90s in my neighbourhood who are housebound and have no visitors. They thought I was doing them a favour but, in fact, they were doing me a huge favour by allowing me to enter their lives and home for that hour.

The second thing I did to get by was to read Sian Williams' book called *Rise*. She is a well-known television journalist and in her book she talks about the deep inner growth that happens from adversity as she came to terms with cancer. For me it was reassuring to know after reading this book that

I was doing all the right things and I was on track, yet why does the ground beneath me disappear? I guess this too is part of the journey.

I know I am not done and I probably will never be done with missing my father and missing the love we shared. And I won't apologise for that either.

My best friend said the other day that 'happy memories are like gold dust amidst life's challenges' and that is so true. It is the gold dust that gives us purpose and meaning. The love we receive from those closest to us should never be underestimated, it is the gold dust we will miss when we part company and it is the memories of those happy times that becomes our lifeline to keep us going when the going gets tough.

Having got through Christmas Day my next challenge in two days is my father's anniversary. For this day the plan is fluid. I will do what I can to get through with the help of some kind friends. I have not been able to plan this day with any great detail. I am wise enough to know that sometimes I just have to let it be and let go of planning and resisting.

To conclude, I come out of this three-year personal journey of mine bruised, washed and battered, yet strong and determined. Nothing will faze me as I know I have my father's invincible spirit and appreciation of life. This life is a gift, we are here to grow and make this world a better place. Our individual contribution, no matter how small, can make a difference to us and to those around us. I don't know about tomorrow but I am grateful about yesterday and today.

If you are reading this and are on your own challenging journey may you have the strength to keep going. Don't compromise, just be yourself and respect yourself, the rest will come together.

My tips:
- Plan ahead if possible to get by the key days.
- It is okay to retreat.

Peace be with you.

DMP

Day 2,000 and the Anniversary...

January 6, 2017

In the last week I marked my dad's third death anniversary and hit day 2,000.

In a couple of days it will be exactly three years since the funeral. Why do I still remember the number of days and the dates? The dates are just etched in my head, I can't help it.

I had all the grab handles removed from my dad's bathroom and the house yesterday. This wasn't timed but it happened on day 2,000. There were mixed feeling with this: was it the right thing to do and am I actually doing this! All the handles I personally bought. The joiner asked if I had been present when they had been installed, 'Of course', I said. All of the 'work' was done in a state of emergency. I was doing everything to help my dad get around the house as independently as possible and he appreciated it too. He would be so happy yet very tired when in the last days he could still walk from the bathroom to the conservatory holding on to the grab handles, which, by the way, were all located on the right-hand side as my dad only had the use of his right hand following the stroke. My adorable dad would walk with a sense of achievement just like a child and he never, ever gave up no matter how frustrating and tiring it was for him.

It was his spirit that I love and still admire. Maybe a bit of his spirit has rubbed off on me, well I hope so anyway.

With all the handles off, my initial reaction when the joiner asked if I was happy with how he had tried to fill the holes with a similar colour to the tiles and wall paint was, 'It is okay'. No matter what I will always see those dots on the walls and remember where the grab handles were. My next job of course was to make sure the handles were going to a good home, so I rang a charity I volunteer for and they have agreed to re-use them for the many senior citizens in our local area which the charity supports.

So that is the story of the grab handles, but I have so many of my father's belongings that I need to re-home and I keep saying to myself I will get to that task when I am good and ready. You'd think after three years I ought to be ready!

As for the dreaded third anniversary it felt like the hardest for me. I was just not in the mood to celebrate my dad's life. I was thinking, yes his passing at the grand old age of ninety-five was right but I miss my best buddy terribly and no, I don't feel so cheerful after all.

It has been a while since I have had a good cry but I was so deeply sad on the day of the anniversary that I went into emotional meltdown. On reflection I am stunned but I can still feel this as I write this. The next day I met a friend. I am not sure what came over me but for the first time in three years I actually sobbed my heart out for a good ten minutes. My friend said I have been trying so hard to keep things together so that the grieving continues. This is probably true, I have had no choice but to be strong and carry on. I have read quite a bit about loss and grief so there is plenty of evidence, including my own first-hand experience, that we find ourselves in this new territory for which we have no training manual. We think we know how to live but learning to live after the death of a significant loved one is not something we actually know how to deal with.

My friend said we slip and slide, and again we go on. That is also true. Compared to the suffering we are surrounded by I tell myself I am grateful for the years of love and happiness I shared with my amazing father. My rational head understands that perfectly but when it comes to the heart and the soul it is a totally different matter entirely. What took me by surprise was the sobbing, and that too after three years, was I really still holding on to so much pain? I must be, where else did this come from?

My dad often asked me how I would deal with his death. My response was always an over confident response that I would be fine and that I would just get on with it. The truth was the opposite. This is my very own Robben Island journey. Yes, it is in no way as hard as Nelson Mandela's journey but hard nonetheless for me. The paradox of all this is that I have grown through my pain and I have a bit more wisdom and enlightenment (though I am sure my dad will say, 'You have a long way to go dear daughter') mixed with a bit of recklessness. I say recklessness because I say to myself I have been through the worst kind of pain, nothing now can ever beat me down. The paradox is strength vs vulnerability. What a fantastic contrast. Still I look back on the past three years and say I wouldn't have had it any other way, just as I would not have wanted to love my father any less. Pain of separation is the price we pay for love and as they say it is better to have loved and lost than not loved at all.

If you are reading this for some comfort I am no expert but I can say this much, it is the painful episodes in our life which make us appreciate the goodness in people and the universe so pain is just as much as necessary as joy. In dealing with pain we have to be true to ourselves and deal with it in our own unique way. There is no right or wrong way but we find our own way of coping and it definitely helps if we are blessed with good people in our lives, I certainly am.

Peace be with you.

DMP

My Dad's 99th Birthday!

April 26, 2017

Here I am after what seems ages. Feeling melancholy though I know I have a lot to be thankful for and that my glass is half full.

Four days ago it would have been my dad's 99th birthday. He wanted to make a century but died at ninety-five. Part of me feels my dad has never left me for he's still a huge part of who I am. Then part of me feels how many more days must I live without him. He was and still is the person who inspires me to be at my best. I now realise I did not appreciate the magnitude of his important presence in my life until after his death. I never thanked him enough when he was alive or appreciated the many millions of things he did for my benefit. I took him for granted.

Regrets and gratitude, we are left with mixed feelings. If I say I miss him it appears he's not in my life but he is. Mostly now when I think of him I smile with pride, I am so glad I am his daughter. I have been going through some obstacles, which often we all have to face, and it is during these times I miss coming home to him, putting my head on his shoulder and not saying a word, for he would understand the workings of my mind. He would put his hand on my head and I would feel so safe and at home. I miss his loving touch on my head and will do for the rest of my life. Nobody will love me the way he does.

We often communicated without words and we understood one another. I guess that is the language of love, trust and something awesomely deep between two souls.

On a positive note, just before my dad's birthday I decided I would mark the day by inviting some friends for a little get-together. The day before I went to the supermarket in preparation of the event and the supermarket bill came to £99.95. At first I did not notice anything untoward then I thought, my dad passed away at ninety-five and tomorrow he would have been ninety-nine. Whether that was a sign or not, I looked up at the skies and said 'thank you'.

On the day itself though, I was feeling numb. I braced myself to put on a good show as I was the host and had to do my best. I went to the local hospice with a cake. I actually went to meet my bereavement counsellor there but instead we ended up in the canteen where I cut the cake and it was quite a sight. Around twenty visitors and staff enjoyed the cake. This was totally unplanned as people helped themselves to the tiny pieces of cake. I was asked about my dad and it really felt good. Something beautiful came about without any effort at all!

Later my friends came home to help me mark the day. It was a good day; we all enjoyed the good company and food. Considering how I felt to begin with it went well. As I reflected on the day, I was in it but felt I was not in it, if that makes sense.

The day was so full on that I did not get the chance to have a one-to-one with my dad (as if he is alive) or even open and read the card to him that I had written to him! Still it was a good way to celebrate his 99th birthday. I am sure he was looking down on us all and smiling away with some degree of amusement and pride.

The next day, after putting the house back together, I put the radio on only for Tony Blackburn to announce the last song of his programme. It was a duet by a father and daughter, Frank and Nancy Sinatra, singing 'Something

Stupid'. I thought, oh my God my dad is reminding me that he loves me. I know it is a romantic song but I don't care - it was sung by a father and daughter and that sign was pretty awesome and meaningful to me. My father and I together were a formidable duo, even in business we worked together in complete harmony.

So, here I am having got through his 99th birthday without him. I am still here standing and seemingly managing with the challenges of life. How I feel inside is only probably apparent to someone who has lost a much loved one.

My thought of my journey thus far is that one does not recover or even feel better after the death of a significant loved one, especially, in my case, the death of an only parent. However, one is able to put on a brave face and give a jolly good impression that life is absolutely fine. As death is part of life we have the choice to accept it with grace and a degree of audacity.

I will end on the note by saying that if someone is on a similar journey to mine, hang in there. Your love for your loved one and their love for you will help you through, and there are lots of kind people around you, be it family, friends and complete strangers who will give you a helping hand when you are down on your knees. You will look back and know for sure that your loved one is very much still with you and will always be with you no matter what. You just have to get used to feeling their presence and seeing them through the eyes of your soul.

Peace be with you.

DMP

Father's Day Again...

June 13, 2017

This Sunday will be my fourth Father's Day without my dad. I am approaching this day with dread and gratitude in equal measure. As time goes by the gut wrenching pain and heartache are still palpable just as they are indescribable, yet I go on, where who knows and why, well, that is another question in itself!

There is this acute hole in my being, well, in my soul and in my heart even though I feel and know that my father has not really left me at all. It is getting used to his physical absence and so much more. Sometimes the pain hits you right at the core of your being. I can be anywhere, at work, at home, walking, watching the TV or even looking at the sky. It just comes from nowhere and knocks me off my track and there I go again, in a place where I do not want to be but glad I can still visit it sometimes. I sense a wobble and depending on where I am and what I am supposed to be doing I compose myself then carry on.

I do have many a good day when I feel on top of the world because I know I was the lucky one to have had the joy and love of such a great man. Yes, I had the privilege of walking to the top of the summit with him. I loved him so much and he loved me, it sounds like this has changed, it hasn't but I sometimes have to remind myself of the times when we were actually together in one room having a discussion on a fascinating subject then concluding what a joy it was to share our thoughts with one another. We got each other completely and I so miss that feeling!

He was a visionary ahead of his time. He was old enough

to remember seeing the first motor vehicle arrive in his home town and young enough at the age of ninety-five to tell me to expand the screen on my smart phone so he could see a picture clearly! Yes, that was my father and I am so proud of that fact.

I tell myself to focus on the glass half full school of thought but sometimes, try as I may, that heaviness is there which I can't shake off. After a while you stop sharing how you feel because it is hard for most to understand. I am fortunate I still have a handful of people in my life who do get it. But I am my worst critic. I wonder if I am self indulgent or wallowing in my grief but really I am not. Parents die, that is the natural order of things, and children move on. Shouldn't I too?

There are moments I really miss him. I took the day off to watch the general election results. I missed him so terribly because we both would normally listen to the election results on Radio 4 all night. We shared our interest in politics. I so wanted to sit with him but he wasn't there. Then yesterday my neighbour said I was a chip off the old block. That was so nice to hear but I wanted him to be present and to see the pride on my face.

Then there are random moments like walking into work when I visualise him walking next to me on my left side because on the odd occasion we did walk together. My dad was a fast walker and I was always playing catch up and he always insisted on walking by the side of the road, his way of protecting me. Then it dawns on me that I am, in fact, walking alone.

Two weeks ago I completed the Yorkshire Three Peaks Challenge; it was a big deal to me. Twelve hours of walking and I am not fond of trekking. I walked into the house, wanted to shout and tell him of my achievement but he wasn't there. The tears of joy or sadness still roll down my face, not as often as before but it still happens when I least expect and there's me thinking I am the Queen of Grief! I found myself searching for the Union Jack which I knew my dad had in the study. I wanted it to use it at the World Triathlon last Sunday. It hit me how organised he kept the study and the filing cabinet. Everything is meticulously filed and stored in the right place.

I know it is only three years, five months and thirteen days since he died but he is still a huge part of my world. Without him I am lost but in a strange way I am slowly finding myself.

This year I have not made any plans to mark Father's Day though I have been aware of its arrival for some time. It's as though I feel paralysed in grief. Sounds heavy and sad I know but it is what it is.

I know exactly how I marked the last three Father's Days and I am not sure I can surpass what I did last year when I had a tattoo done on my left arm, but this year I just hope I get through this day intact without losing sight of the good things in my life, and there are many. Perhaps there is no miracle cure and no right or wrong. We all just have to help each other muddle along and get by!

To anyone out there reading this blog, if you are a dad or you have a dad make the most of your time with your loved ones. It is the memories we create in our living world that helps those left behind. Don't miss out on the chance of telling your dad how much you love him and appreciate his presence in your life. I would do anything to do just that right now.

Peace be with you.

DMP

This Selfish Grief Of Mine

This selfish grief of mine
My basket of burden is filled with grief and my loss
It is so heavy to carry although this road I must cross
This selfish grief of mine is mine and mine alone

This path through life feels unbearable at times
And I don't have the strength for this mountain to climb

This pain goes so deep right down to my core
And a relationship like ours deserves a pause

Grief is so very personal and so natural indeed
To not grieve would be to say it matters not

My Dad my friend my mentor my life
My ties with him will not be severed in any life

I lived with this great man for 2,600 weeks
And it is only 20 weeks without him

Patience is needed to carry this loss I feel
A shoulder to lean on someday I will heal

God sent my friends and spirits unknown
So I won't carry this basket of burden forever alone

This basket of burden is filled with grief and my loss
It's so heavy to carry but this road I must cross
This selfish grief of mine is mine and mine alone

DMP
2nd June 2014

Adapted from a poem by Debbie, March 2010 from www.familyfriends.com

3 Years, 8 Months and 4 Days

September 3, 2017

It has been a while since my last blog. I have been thinking what to say, so much has happened and there is so much I still wish to discuss with my dad. Three years and eight months sounds like a long time but to me it seems only yesterday my father passed.

The last days and moments are etched in my mind though I try not to dwell on those days. My father made me and I will always be thankful that he was such a big part of my life.

After all this time I know one thing, the void left by my father's death is so huge that nothing will replace this big hole in my being BUT that's absolutely fine too.

He lives on in my life and in everything I do. I write this blog from Dubai, my father and I visited this same place some six years ago. Though at the time he was in a wheelchair, what I remember distinctly is that he was in his element and, given the chance even in that condition, he probably would have travelled the world with me because I know he lived for me.

When we came last time I hired a private yacht much to his delight. I repeated the same journey this time with a feeling that he was watching over me saying, 'Enjoy, I am still with you.'

I went deep-sea diving today, first time ever, and I was thinking what he would have made of that. I can hear him saying, 'Go my daughter do what pleases you.' I was out of my comfort zone and I doubt I would have had the courage to do this before. Some of my friends have commented on the change they see in me, and though I think I am the same person, one thing I know now is that I am more willing to take a chance. Unlike my dad, who was not shy of taking risks, I always took a cautious approach to life. Something has changed.

Grief is like a slow dance. At first you have no idea how to survive/dance then you begin to get into the rhythm of it. After a while you learn to see what you have achieved rather than what still needs fine tuning. I don't want to associate my father's memory with pain and sadness, oh no, he means joy and life to me. He means living a life with purpose and zest.

He had his fair share of tragedies having lost his wife to TB and their two young children when he was only twenty-seven. He did not give up on life, he lived, but I know whenever he spoke of his first wife he did so with so much love and fondness. He remarried and had a new family but his first wife lived on with him. Even now, when I think of my dad and where he might be and what he might be doing, I instantly think he must be with his first wife, Rewa, just waiting for me to arrive on the scene.

If there is one thing that has helped me to get to this point it is the knowledge that I am his daughter, I cannot afford to give up on life. I am blessed I have friends who are more like family. I am surrounded by kind souls who care for me. I am grateful for their presence in my life.

Dancing through grief is where I feel I am now, but at the start I was totally broken to the point that I did not know if I would make it thought the first year, never mind three years on. So, grief and loss of any significance teaches us about our own strength and resilience. It is a slow dance. At first you do not know the steps then slowly with patience and practise you get the hang of the basic steps, but each time

you learn something new about the universe, about your love and about yourself.

For me my father's death was a turning point for me to get to know me.

In times of crisis or doubt I always remember my father's words, which were, 'Live with a lion's heart unafraid of anything or anyone. Life is a gift we are meant to be kind to ourselves and to others.'

I know he is watching over me, protecting me, guiding me and spurring me on to live life to the full and that is what I intend to do. That will be my way of expressing my gratitude to him for making me who I am today.

If you happen to stumble across this post because you are going through your own journey of loss and pain, please be kind to yourself. Losing a significant loved one doesn't break you it makes you. You will be amazed by your own courage.

My tips:
- stretch yourself.
- be fearless.

Peace be with you always.

DMP

It's Exhausting...

September 28, 2017

In three months time it will be four years. The beginning of autumn and the early dark evenings is a reminder that I am approaching the fourth death anniversary. It's heavy.

Somebody asked why I was not attending to a matter that would save me money and I replied that I was just getting by with life, I haven't got the energy. It is hard perhaps to see but it is so exhausting living without my dad, I just do what I must in order to get by on a day-to-day basis. I only know on reflection how much effort I have to make to put on a near normal appearance in every aspect of my life. I have become so good at faking it that even I don't recognise the effort I am making most of the time, so I can hardly expect that of others.

As I approach this day, other anniversary memories of the end come flooding back. It doesn't seem like four years, in fact, I've never been so aware and present in my life as I have been since my father's death. Though I always feel grateful for the life that I have and the experiences, this undoubtedly has been the toughest journey of my life for sure.

I often wonder how amazing others are when coping with the loss of a significant person in their life. It is a silent, solitary and very private journey. You only open up to those you trust, will understand or genuinely care about you.

Grief is a teacher of our own strength and is a shocking awakening reminder, almost like the blow of a blunt knife, of our own fragility, frailty and vulnerability. You go from being this 'always strong' person to 'my gosh she's still grieving'!

I only speak of my experience and I know many have been through so much more but there is no comparison to be had. Our grief and our experience of loss is as unique as our relationship with our loved one. Of course added to that is our own personality, perspective and uniqueness, then there are what we perceive as the expectations. The only expectations we need to manage are our own!

When we see someone with a broken leg immediately we feel sympathy. Well, this is a broken heart; we must be gentle and kind to our soul.

My mind was in agony thinking about those parents whose children were buried when a school collapsed in Mexico City following the earthquake. Their pain doesn't bear thinking about. I have learnt when we have no words that can soothe an aching heart a glance of understanding is better. A slight human touch on the shoulder is better than no acknowledgement of their loss.

Sometimes I just want to curl up in bed and not wake up to face another day of having to make an effort. That feeling doesn't last very long. If we are alive it is a blessing. Also, I am glad for this experience even though it can be exhausting at times.

I want to end on a positive note as even in our darkest moments there's something to be grateful about. Victor Frankl, a professor of neurology and psychiatry who spent three years in Auschwitz and other concentration camps, wrote in his book **Man's Search for Meaning** that even in the depth of great despair and hopelessness it is possible to find a reason to be grateful for. The great challenge for man is to find meaning in his or her life. According to him this meaning can come from either work, doing something meaningful, in love – that is caring for another – and in courage in difficult times. He says you cannot control what happens to you in life, but you can always control what you will feel and do about what happens to you. In short, we always have the free will to choose how we respond to a given situation and that is not something anyone can take away from us.

I still live hoping my father will be proud of me. Though he is not on planet Earth it still matters to me what he thinks of me and how I make him feel. Hard to understand my thinking but I believe the soul is eternal, so then it follows that our connection is not severed by death.

So, to anyone out there, for the sake of your loved one – be it your mum, dad, partner, husband, wife, child or sibling – don't give up and don't give in. Live on and make them proud.

Peace be with you.

DMP

Almost 4 Years

November 27, 2017

I am close to the fourth anniversary of my father's death. It is three years, ten months and twenty-eight days to be precise since he died. I look at myself and I am amazed I am here still and that, too, in one piece.

If I could I would remove the month of December from the calendar for my own selfish reasons as I still find it hard to engage in the seasonal festivities. The thought of putting the Christmas tree up and the sight of Christmas trees in the malls feels like an irritant. I mean I still cannot go to M & S and if I did I would avoid walking past the men's department as this would be a reminder of the many things I can no longer buy for my dad. The sound of Christmas songs and the hustle and bustle of Christmas shoppers all still provoke a very intense feeling in me, so much so that I just want to disappear from the land of living…

Last weekend I found myself going over my journals and in particular the notes I made just before my father's passing and just after. As I read them I felt sad that I was so heartbroken, desolate and bereft. I have never been one to be pitiful and neither was my father. We just got on with things but losing my dad cracked me open completely. At one stage I had noted that I was like a vase broken into a million pieces and hard to put back together. I have been mended in a manner of speaking. To the outside world I do look the same but to me I hardly recognise me. Here I am about to attempt my first full London Marathon, something I would not have ever contemplated before. The rebuilding of me is something that took me by surprise but I am very proud that I managed to put myself together, albeit with inner scars, but there is more work to be done for sure. Though it has been tough I would not change a thing.

Inside I still feel broken but outwards I have moved forward, but when I look at myself I do not recognise this 'new' me. Adversity and suffering in many ways makes us more grateful for what we have. I am deeply grateful to all those who have been on my side supporting me and encouraging me along the way. Yes, the last three years and ten months have been like a long full marathon. Hard work and at times impossible, not to mention very exhausting, but I am getting there. I would probably say I am 25 per cent into the 26.2 miles journey.

While I am grateful for everything I still miss my father so much. I miss our long conversations, I miss his smiling face, and I miss his approvals and disapprovals. I know he would be very proud of me in how I have conducted myself since his death. He always said he had complete faith in my abilities but while before his death I was super confident that I would manage life, after my dad's death that notion went out of the window as I crumbled to pieces. So, what the last three years and ten months has taught me is that I should not believe I know everything about me. I don't know my full potential and I do not know how fragile I am. I have seen my most vulnerable side and I have seen my resilient side. We are ill equipped to deal with death either and also because we do not know the magnitude of our loss until we walk the journey.

I know it is not yet December and I sense a wobble so I expect some turbulence ahead. I have to remind myself that as invincible as I am I cannot shed the heaviness all the time. I have come a long way but grief is just a reminder of the depth of our love. I love my father and I have proved it to myself that I am through and through my father's daughter.

Thank you for reading this blog. If I can offer some comfort to anyone out there on a similar journey it is just this: trust yourself and do what feels right, the rest will come together for we are far stronger than we think we are.

Peace be with you.

DMP

Year 4...

December 19, 2017

As I approached December I did so with a degree of dread but thus far I have got through without crumbling.

Wayne Dyer, the esteemed philosopher, said: 'What we see is not real what we don't see is!'

I definitely feel my dad is with me but I can't prove it. I don't need to, I just know. This month has been momentous. I leave my job with a firm I have been with for almost seventeen years. My work has been a saving grace but leaving feels a necessary part of my healing. My colleagues have been absolutely awesome. They have given me so much emotional support.

This month I also started training for the London Marathon, so far thanks to my great coach I am on track in spite of the cold weather. And of course I also mark yet another Christmas, another anniversary and another new year. The Christmas tree is up looking glorious as usual. My dad would always switch the lights on but I do it now on his behalf. Our live Christmas tree sits in the front garden, my father always thought a well decorated tree would bring a smile to those passing our home. That thought helps me through and one thing I have found is that all the rituals of marking Christmas, like giving a present to the bin man and the postie, feels a necessary part of life. This is the one time in the year where we can show our appreciation to others so why miss the chance.

I am quietly optimistic I will get through the next few days emotionally in one piece.

I read in the early days that when we approach an

anniversary or a special day it is helpful if we plan ahead. Take it from me, it helps.

I am also acutely aware that we are not really in control. I remember when my dad passed on 30th December, it was 2.20pm, a clear and crisp winter afternoon. As soon as I knew he had passed I felt this overwhelming sense of relief and gratitude to the Lord. Relief because I would never have to worry about him suffering anymore. Gratitude that he died with me holding his hand and in the presence of those people whom he loved. My final words before he passed was that I was handing his hand into the hands of the Lord, as I write this I feel those exact emotions but I still think it is a blessing that his time on earth ended just as he wished. He died in his own home with me beside him.

Every challenge and every soul I encounter in this physical life is a necessary part of my journey and a blessing.

A close friend of mine recently gave me a plaque which read:

'In every ending there is a new beginning.'

I am beginning to realise how true that is.

If you are reading this post I wish you a very Merry Christmas and a peaceful New Year. I hope you find your own garden of oasis. Peace resides in us if we find that first we can see it outside as well.

Peace be with you.

DMP

The Impact Of Grief...

February 12, 2018

Four years on since my father's death I know I have done really well to survive but sometimes, when I least expect it, grief knocks on the door of my soul and hits me sideways.

The other day while travelling on the train I had a shaky moment when I saw a gentleman wearing a dark grey winter coat just like the one my dad had. I had a wobble then I gathered myself, well what choice did I actually have?

I thought wrongly that I understand all there is to grief. After all it has been my companion for the past few years. Yes, another one of my 'I know it all, I will be fine' phases. Truth is each day I learn something new.

So I turn to those who are better placed than I to define what grief is…

Grief is a tidal wave that overtakes you, smashes down
upon you with unimaginable force, sweeps you up into its
darkness, where you tumble and crash against unidentifiable
surfaces, only to be thrown out on an unknown beach,
bruised, reshaped…Grief will make a new person out of
you, if it doesn't kill you in the making.

Stephanie Ericsson

'Bereavement is the deepest initiation into the mysteries
of human life, an initiation more searching and profound
than even happy love.'

Dean Inge

'If you look deeply into the palm of your hand, you will see
your parents and all generations of your ancestors. All of
them are alive in this moment. Each is present in your body.
You are the continuation of each of these people.'

Thich Nhat Hanh

From my very short journey I know this much: love and grief go hand in hand just like day and night. If we are blessed to have loved someone so deeply and they us then it is inevitable that their physical absence will cause sorrow and pain. Coming to terms with the death of a loved one or as some will say rather harshly 'moving on' is a process. I do not believe it is possible to move on but I do feel we have a choice to move forward and do so with some gratitude and dignity. If we do not succumb to the sorrow of grief and keep living it is a fitting tribute to the love we share.

Something deep drives me to keep moving forward that is not linked to power, money, ego or vanity, it is the fact that I am my father's daughter and I want him to be proud of me still.

The quote below from Maya Angelou is how I feel right now.

> 'My mission in life is not merely to survive, but to thrive; and to do so with some passion, some compassion, some humour and some style'... and I would add some panache!

I hope this gives some hope to anyone out there reading this blog, please don't give up, you have to believe the sun will shine again. Travel this journey at your pace. This is one journey we cannot be prescriptive about.

Peace be with you.

DMP

1,554 Days On...

April 2, 2018

A quote by T.S. Elliot inspired me to write this post today.

> *'We shall not cease from exploration*
> *And the end of all our exploring*
> *Will be to arrive where we started*
> *And know the place for the first time.'*

He further advised to find the still point of the turning world.

I started this blog to help me and those on a similar journey to try to make sense of the death of a father.

It is 1,554 days or four years, three months and two days since my dad's freedom and my journey to find the lost me.

Someone quite rightly said grief creates an extraordinary energy. Those who really knew my dad and witnessed our beautiful relationship will know how much he meant to me. He was my father and my best friend. Still is.

In the early days I thought I'd lost my dad. We tend to associate our existence with our physical form but we are as Dr. Wayne Dyer said, 'spiritual beings on earth having a human experience and not humans having a spiritual experience'.

I realise now my dad still inspires me to raise my game and to be a better human being. Well, I strive to anyhow.

It would be remiss of me not to acknowledge and appreciate all those good people who have come into my life since my father's death and at the right time as I was broken open. As I fell I was fortunate to have been caught by another and there were times when I was in free fall.

These kind souls just stepped into my life and made my journey bearable.

Something I learnt from my father was no matter how dismal a situation appears don't give up and don't give in. At times I had to dig deep and really push myself to get through the day in hand. The lesson I learnt from my dad has stood me in good stead and in nineteen days' time I will mark what would have been my dad's 100th birthday and I will also embark on my biggest emotional and physical challenge yet. Yes, I have the audacity to think I can run the London Marathon 26.2 miles!

I hope to achieve this with a bit of help from my dad, the universe and my great friends.

There will be many runners there like me who will be running a full marathon for the first time and they too will have their own personal stories spurring them on.

For me this all feels surreal. I'm still amazed I've survived 1,554 days and more amazed that I'm here.

Regardless of the outcome of the challenge ahead, I thank all those kind people who've helped me get here. My friends you know who you are, thank you for being by my side when my world crumbled many times over and still does. Thank you to my brilliant coach who has selflessly supported me and encouraged me every step of the way. There have been perfect strangers who have unknowingly helped; so many of you have played a part in my getting to this point, including my past and present work colleagues who've just been amazingly supportive. The list of kind people is endless.

I have come to realise that I started this journey of trying to make sense of my life without my dad and trying to find me but I have gained so much along the way. We are resilient and we love. Love gives us strength and courage but it also makes us vulnerable. I have learnt to open my heart and to be thankful for all that is. I will not stop exploring and I never want to stop being grateful for the joy and the heartache because it is this that makes us whole. Amidst the chaos we must find the still point of this turning world and feel wow, amazing grace, thank you God.

Peace be with you.

DMP

100 Not Out...

April 28, 2018

In my mind my dad is 100 not out. I marked this milestone in a slightly unusual way. My dad would have turned 100 on 21st April, and he would definitely have approved with the way I went about celebrating his big birthday.

On his birthday I would normally have had a small get-together at home but this year I didn't have the time.

On the 21st April I set off on what was my biggest emotional and physical challenge ever. Something I'd been preparing for since November. I was on my way to run the London Marathon. Even when I say this it feels surreal, I mean me run 26.2 miles/42 kms? It sounds bizarre because up and until 2013 the only runs I had done were fun runs and a few half marathons when I was in my twenties.

The training and preparation for this challenge was huge. The only thing I focused on during the past six months was work and training. My training was the biggest and most important project, everything else took second place.

It was a Saturday. I got ready, sat in front of my dad (his photo of course) wished him a happy birthday, thanked him for guiding me thus far and told him I was getting him a medal as a gift. Went to the train station to meet up with my three friends who had kindly agreed to accompany me to London, including my fabulous coach, and got the surprise of my life. Two other lovely souls who have also been my ardent friends were waiting to give me a grand send off, they held a great big orange banner right in the middle of the train station. The banner said: 'London Marathon May the force be with you!' I was overwhelmed and speechless by this kindness.

Words still fail to describe how taken aback I still am by all the support and kindness these friends so generously gave to me. I wasn't alone in London, my friends were with me. They gave me their time, energy and support and I shall forever be in their debt. They were there waiting to cheer me on at miles six, twelve and twenty-one, as well as at the end. How blessed I am, I know. The many messages of support and encouragement was them taking the place of my dad to spur me on.

Then we took the train to London during which my coach briefed me and gave me a pep talk and I felt like a true athlete, though deep down I kept thinking I'm a pretender! I couldn't have wished for a more devoted coach. He was with me every step of the way encouraging me to raise my game and was monitoring my progress as he knew how important it was that I completed this challenge.

My dad and her majesty the Queen share the same birthday, and the Queen opened the London Marathon on 22nd April 2018. So that was a great omen and start. All my training was done in cold weather conditions but on the day the hottest ever London Marathon was predicted. And it was, twenty-five degrees scorching hot. Last minute my gear had to be changed and so did my strategy.

It's the 28th today and it still feels incredible that I ran a marathon!

Without much conscious planning on my part the hotel we stayed at was only fifteen minutes' walking distance to the start line. My coach and I got there, on the way he reminded me to focus and go at a steady pace. He believed in me but was equally on tenterhooks given the distance involved. I mean the longest distance I'd run until that day was seventeen miles never mind 26.2!

For me, aside from the fact that I had set this personal challenge, riding on that were all those kind people who had generously donated to St. Gemma's Hospice for whom I was raising funds. This is a brilliant hospice which provides end-of-life care and fabulous support to the families. So far monies raised are around £1,867.

The gun went and the run I had dreamt of doing started in earnest. I was among 40,000 runners, all running for their very personal reasons. I knew I had to respect the distance and the opportunity I had been blessed with. My aim was to enjoy myself, go at a steady pace and be proud of myself. Seven hours, eighteen minutes and eight seconds later, I was having my picture taken having completed my first ever marathon, the London Marathon 2018, with the medal around my neck. I looked up in the sky and said, 'Thank you Father, and thank you God, for helping me to get here.'

Looking back I can say everything unfolded in a magical way. Even my energy and stamina was exceptional given the distance. I looked quite alive at the end though this could be the joy of completing this feat and a sense of relief. I knew whatever the outcome my dad would be proud of me but what struck me was the love and support I received from everyone. Not finishing the run was not an option. This was a magnificent achievement considering my journey over the last four years and four months since my dad's death. They say if it doesn't break you grief will make you stronger. In my case I was broken but slowly the pieces of my life are being put together. I am the same but I am a bit more aware than before. I wouldn't go as far as saying I'm enlightened but I've learnt a lot. This achievement was a team effort.

My dad died at the grand old age of ninety-five and though he's no more it was important to me to celebrate his 100th birthday in style because he never lost his zest for life.

I see him willing me on to LIVE and THRIVE.

The run-up to April has been emotionally trying. My final gift to my dear dad on his birthday is me fulfilling his last wish, to come to Mauritius, which is where I am writing this post from. I am sitting on the edge of the Indian Ocean on a sandy beach at a tiny exclusive resort on the east of Mauritius.

My trip here is a pilgrimage and homage to this great man whom I'm proud to call my father. We shared a deep connection, very loving and very respectful. Completing the London Marathon and my trip to Mauritius is my tribute to my father and his life.

Happy birthday dear Pops!!

If you are grieving for the loss of a special and significant person, please don't lose heart. Your love is bigger than your loss. They would want you to live life to the full. So do it and do it on your terms…

Peace be with you.

DMP

4 Years and 6 Months!

June 25, 2018

It is precisely four years five months and twenty-six days or rather 1,638 days since my dad died. I am not still grieving but yes I know the days and hours I have survived without him. When I say without him I mean without his physical presence. I have trained my heart and mind to feel his presence most of the time and on the odd occasion I fall, and still do, but I find him again. Yesterday I went to the park by the lake where I have scattered my dad's ashes. and sat down, as it was a beautiful warm day, to enjoy nature at its glorious best when a thought occurred. I asked myself, can I remember the times we sat together, the times we walked together, the times we laughed together, the times we sat down and ate together, and the list went on. The answer was I do remember those days when he and I used to walk around this very park. We would sit on the bench together but I can't remember the last time he and I sat down to eat together. I then thought I hope I never forget those happy moments we had because it is his smiling eyes and his smiling face that keeps me going. It is those happy memories that help us to keep marching forward.

Though it is almost four and a half years since his death, every day without fail I have written a note to my dad. These are not letters to my dad but my daily conversation. It is here that I tell him about what makes me smile and what worries I carry. Sometimes I get into a sticky patch and I think if he was here I would have asked him for his advice. If I can't think of what he might have said I just leave a note to my dad to help me find the answer. The void left by his death is there, I cannot deny it.

The difficulty with us humans is that we tend to only recognise the physical world and ignore the unseen, however, nobody has seen love; it is felt. We love the person whom we think is the body when it is, in fact, the soul we are in love with.

The person who has had the biggest influence in my life was and is still my father. We shared a journey together that fills my heart with gratitude in abundance. The last four years and almost six months have been a period when I have learnt the most about me. It has been the most difficult period yet the most important period of my life. I am glad I had him as my dad and I am so glad I have been on this journey. My life has turned upside down and still is upside down but I am happy that I have learnt to see the world from a different perspective!

To all those hurting and missing the loss of their parent, remember death does not tear us apart from our loved ones it brings us closer together in ways we weren't before.

> *'Don't grieve. Anything you lose comes round in another form.'*
> (Rumi)

Peace be with you.

DMP

Broken Open...

August 23, 2018

It's been on my mind to post a note, only I needed some headspace to stand back and reflect on my journey since my dad's death. I'm reflecting with a sense of gratitude.

Love does not have a best before date. It just is. My relationship with my dad is the same. He still inspires me to raise my game and he's still proud of me. I just know.

I had never felt broken until my dad passed. When this happens our pride may take a bashing and our vulnerability is put on display, but so what? When we are going through pain, we may want to give up hope and give in to despair, but many brave souls have gone on this journey before us so we can take heart from their journey.

We have within us the resilience which comes from the strength of our deep love between us and our departed loved one and between us and the universe.

To walk through the fog of grief and to not give in to despair is a challenge. Rumi's words offer some comfort. Even when you feel you are breaking into a million pieces believe you'll make it like many pilgrims before you. Never give up, your love is precious and this will keep you strong. Instead allow your heart to be open, break open and you'll gain an understanding that will lead you to feel free and grow into a more compassionate being.

I won't say it's easy but there is hope. Love is eternal it is not restricted by form. We feel its power and we know.

My father was a liberated soul. Despite many obstacles in life, and he had more than his fair share, he never used that as an excuse. He kept going and so must I.

'Drum sounds rise on the air,
and with them my heart.
A voice inside the beat says,
I know you are tired,
but come.
This is the way.'

Rumi

So, to those on a similar journey, please keep going. Hope and just be. Be kind to your soul.

Peace be with you.

DMP

57 Months...

October 9, 2018

I heard someone say grief is like glitter, you can never quite get rid of it - no matter how hard you try it is always there. So, for me it is four years, nine months and nine days since my dad passed. Those going through a similar journey will know this journey is excruciatingly hard but we have no choice but to walk through this in our own unique way.

Today I want to touch on the things or shall I say the tools I used to help me during the climb. A snapshot of where I was in the early days will kind of put this into some context. In the early days I felt I was actually going mad. I was offered anti -depressants but I said, 'No, this is grief and it is healthy to process it if I can without a crutch.' I did not know if I could but I wanted to try. The truth is I did not believe I could survive without my dad's physical presence, let alone go past his first death anniversary.

My life ground to a halt amidst a world that was busy moving but I was at a standstill. My life was empty, joyless and without meaning. I felt I was stood in the middle of an earthquake totally exposed to the elements with no one holding my back or even my hand. Alone, fatherless, bereft, and all I wanted was my dad to console me and to tell me I would be okay.

The only person who could possibly get near to me to help me come to terms with my dad's passing was ironically the one person I most yearned for and trusted, and that was my father. I hit the lowest point when one day while walking to work I put a tape measure in my pocket to see if I could climb over a bridge railing. I did nothing of the sort but the measure of my grief was that many of my friends thought I would never, ever 'recover'. I have learnt to better handle how I feel and I have learnt to live with my new life which carries the scars of my journey.

So, from feeling a fatherless orphan (which I still am) I come to the present. I have repeatedly reinvented myself. When you accept your own vulnerability and accept that you are broken you reach a point where you feel you have nothing to lose by taking risks and doing things you never dared to comprehend before you were broken. I have actually walked on hot coal, I've run a marathon and I have left my job twice without another job in place. I have stretched myself.

I have gone from thinking my dad had died and that I had 'lost' him to now believing and knowing that he is walking with me every step of the way. I have not lost him and he has not died. I found this card which perfectly sums up my now and sits on our conservatory wall. The words are: 'I AM WITH YOU ALWAYS'.

He is, I know. And I am glad I know this fact. In my book this is one tiny step to enlightenment. I know I still have a long way to go when it comes to learning the universal truth of my existence.

The tools I have used to help me on this pilgrimage come from learning what others have helpfully shared and also come from my own journey.

1. Rituals – this word sounds rather dogmatic but in its right sense it is not. In our conservatory I have my dad's favourite picture. I light a candle every day. Sometimes I talk to him, sometimes I leave a note asking for his thoughts on a particular issue or sometimes I just sit and thank him in silence.

Sometimes, when I am not in a great mood, I don't say anything and I know he gets me! This practice of lighting a candle and sitting in front of his picture is something I do daily, come rain or shine.

2. Talking to my dad – a good Samaritan-like friend gave me a sympathy card with this lovely poem on the next page by Henry Scott Holland. It took a while to sink in but I understand it. I wake up and say 'good morning' to my dad, and I say 'thank you' and 'good night' also. I come home from work and call him just like I did before to say, 'Dado I am home.' When I am in pain and I really need him I call him at the top of my lungs. I feel now my dad is only a thought away. He feels my pain, my joy and he reads me just like he did when he was in the physical world.

3. Writing – as a lawyer I draft and write for a living but I love words now more than before. They have been my companion. I can pour my heart out, process my feelings and express my gratitude for the everyday comforts and joys that I am blessed with in my journals. Just before my father passed I started to keep a journal. Four years on I have about twenty-five journals because first thing in the morning I write a conversation with my father and sometimes the Lord. Oprah Winfrey often talks about having a gratitude journal. Mine is a mix of reflection and everyday things, the kind of stuff my dad and I would have talked about. Wherever I go I always have my journal to hand. There has not been a day since I have not written. On particularly challenging days I start by writing about it. I make a conscious effort to use only positive words but sometimes it is not possible so I say it how I feel. Putting our thoughts on paper is

Death Is Nothing At All

Death is nothing at all.
I have only slipped away to the next room.
I am I and you are you.
Whatever we were to each other,
That, we still are.

Call me by my old familiar name.
Speak to me in the easy way
which you always used.
Put no difference into your tone.
Wear no forced air of solemnity or sorrow.

Laugh as we always laughed
at the little jokes we enjoyed together.
Play, smile, think of me. Pray for me.
Let my name be ever the household word
that it always was.

Let it be spoken without effect.
Without the trace of a shadow on it.

Life means all that it ever meant.
It is the same that it ever was.
There is absolute unbroken continuity.
Why should I be out of mind
because I am out of sight?

I am but waiting for you.
For an interval.
Somewhere. Very near.
Just around the corner.

All is well.

Nothing is past; nothing is lost. One brief moment and all will be as it was before only better, infinitely happier and forever we will all be one together with Christ.

Henry Scott Holland

therapeutic and I have found it to give me strength and clarity. This habit has been my helpful companion and it is a daily record of how I have walked this journey.
4. Reaching out and volunteering – I thought my profession made me empathetic but actually I learnt to become more compassionate and empathetic after my dad's passing because so many kind souls reached out to me in my hour of need. I now make it my business to reach out to those on a similar journey. Having a small idea of how one may feel all we need to do is not to intrude on someone's private hurt but to just let them know you are there for them. I found in my early days I had a handful of friends who checked in on me just to see I was 'okay' with the full knowledge that I may not respond, but they knew I knew they were there for me if necessary. That knowledge is powerful both for the giver and the recipient. I have volunteered as a mentor to undergraduate law students and have found it has benefited me hugely by this simple act of sharing. I volunteer with Silver Line, which is a charity for isolated senior citizens – again the benefit to me far outweighs anything I may seemingly give. I just completed my seventy-fifth weekly call to a lovely soul.
5. Just be – there are still times when even the most necessary but mundaneness of life becomes impossible to handle. I went from someone who was always on top of her paperwork to having days when I would have unopened post. My Sundays are my sacred day for 'me'. I rest, read, or maybe do nothing and just be. For most of us we usually have a list of

things we need to do. I have come to realise the grief we feel following the passing of a significant loved one is exhausting on many levels. Sheer emotional and physical exhaustion is the best description. Your mind becomes numb, your body feels tired and no matter how often you rest, you still feel like you need more. I usually spot the signs of reaching the about to 'crash' state and I let go in readiness. Reading can be uplifting as well as listening to music. I have had days when I have turned off the phone, the laptop, and laid down with my dad's favourite duvet; feeling him close to me actually helps me to re-energise. When we go through this seismic journey it is imperative that we are kind to ourselves. We need to give ourselves permission to just be and to give ourselves some slack because only we know how we have got from point A to point B. The saying that we can only appreciate another's journey if we have walked in their shoes is spot on here.

6. Walking – in the early days I wasn't working. In fact, aside from looking after me, running a household, sorting the probate and many things one needs to do after the death of a loved one, I did function in an autopilot way experiencing many crashes along the way. These crashes were like going into free fall, losing control with no emergency brakes to stop. For many months I wasn't able to sleep a whole night. Prior to my dad's passing I was like a fire fighter, getting up so many times during the night meant having an uninterrupted night's sleep was a luxury.

You'll get my drift, getting a good night's sleep was my major challenge; consequently I would wake up feeling very lethargic. My father loved walking and until the age of ninety-two he walked every day about four miles so I decided I would follow in his footsteps and I am glad I did. In the early days when I could not stand my own company or felt I was about to break I would just put my coat on and walk, walk and walk for hours on end. Being out in nature feeling the breeze touch my face reminded me I was alive. Seeing trees solid and their magnificent state taught me so much and it kept me going, where, I had no idea back then. I would walk all day to feel physically tired but would come home 'proud' that I had managed to set foot out of the house. That's usually the first battle. No matter how bad we feel, get up, get dressed and get out and do something. Even if you can smile at another and say 'good morning' you have made an effort.

I could not stand the sound of noise and that is still a problem. Going for a long walk in a park looking at the blue sky and feeding the ducks became my purpose. In fact, every weekend in the morning I still attend morning worship, no not in the temple but I go to our local park where I have scattered my dad's ashes, to feed the ducks. I feel I am feeding the hungry ducks but, in fact, they have saved me from me losing myself. Now I walk to and from work so on average I can easily clock up to forty to fifty miles per week of walking. The added benefit of this is fitness and better endurance. We feel better for trying and every little effort helps with our overall wellbeing.

Whether one believes in God or not I do believe there is a supreme power higher than me who guides me and helps me to raise my game. My dad is still the centre of my universe and I am so grateful that he is. I have met God through my father's smiling eyes.

  Until next time I wish you peace and inner joy. Keep walking.

Peace be with you.

DMP

4 Years, 11 Months and 21 Days…

December 21, 2018

Almost five years…

Seemingly a milestone of sorts. To me the time since my dad's passing has been painstakingly slow. My world turned upside down when I became an orphan. Grief affects us all in different ways.

On 16th December 2013, my dad and I went for our last long drive together. Just me and him, the formidable father-daughter duo. I was driving, Dad was in the passenger seat. Both of us grateful to be in each other's company. My dad though, by now incredibly frail, would still say 'yes' to my demands of going for a drive. That was the last time he left home alive. Now I remember that as if it was yesterday.

Almost five years on I have noticed if I have to brake suddenly my left hand goes out as if to protect him in the passenger seat. I am always surprised when this happens because by now I should have got used to my dad not being in the car!

Ever since his death December has not been a month I look forward to. Some grief experts will say the normal grieving period is twelve to eighteen months. He was and still is the person I love the most. I owe all I am today to him so it is hard to not feel his absence, but despite his death his presence in my life is constant. I have not stopped talking to him or telling him how my day went, only difference is I don't hear his voice and I don't hear him call out my name. I still have my dad's mobile number on my mobile and when I feel really down I send a message knowing full well he is not going to reply!

The five years have forced me to re-evaluate my life. I started the journey totally unsure if I would get to even the end of year one. Along the way I have set tiny goals to give me focus and a reason to make life meaningful. If life with my dad was like walking to the summit of the tallest mountain, life after him has been like going downhill with a view to climbing another summit, well at least I hope to before I die.

Grief has the power to strangle your very being but it also has the power to transform your life. My father's love for me was unconditional. He is irreplaceable and the void I feel even now is unlikely to diminish, it just is.

I've learnt that even when we are finding ourselves we can feel better by reaching out to others. But the truth is that it is actually others who help us to keep taking the next step. Imagine learning to walk again. You need patience and you need to make an effort but you also need to be kind to yourself. An army of angels will walk into your life and slowly but surely you will learn to find your bearings, in my case with a bit of help from my friends. I cannot thank enough all those who have walked into my life since my father's death to help me through this maze. Often these are strangers and friends. Yet this is like a very long run. A solitary journey you have to go at your own pace, stop when you need to catch your breath, and keep going when you have a sudden burst of energy. You honestly don't know if you will make the finishing line but you are grateful for all those on the side spurring you on.

If you are on this journey accept this pain with grace, it is healthy to grieve. Don't apologise for how you feel because it's normal to be broken. Grief cracks you open and it makes you vulnerable. That too is normal. If you love deeply you will hurt deeply, that's the deal. So accept it and feel the full brunt of this painful journey. Be proud of your connection with your loved one.

I read a letter from a well-known celebrity who wrote about his take on grief following the death of his teenage son. He said something about reawakening after the calamity. He spoke about the impossible and unspeakable pain that has the potential for a better now leaving us unimaginably changed.

Of course my dad lived a long life yet I feel I have been through the tumble dryer. Bashed and battered but here I am seemingly looking intact.

Thinking of my dad, I have decorated our live Christmas tree in the front of our home as he always wanted to give passing motorists a reason to smile. It took effort because I was not in the mood. I feel melancholy. As always I would like to end this post on a positive note if only because I really do believe that when we do find ourselves digging deep to find us we do find the courage to rise and rise, which we must as this is the best tribute we can give to the person we loved and lost.

I will end this post with the poem I read at my father's funeral and despite the passage of time and the change I have endured my sentiments remain the same.

I thank the poet because these words resonate with my soul.

If you are going through a similar journey I wish you well for the New Year and hope you find the strength to keep going.

Peace be with you.

DMP

The Gift God Gave Me Was You

I will never say goodbye to you, my father,
because I know this is not the end for us to see each other.
You will only be going to a place where there's no pain
suffering.
I am happy for you, for you will be with God.
For now we need to go in separate ways.
I remember how your arms hold me and give me strength.
You were always there to listen, love, and defend me in
everything.
You were my very best friend.
In my triumphs you were always proud.
I'm very grateful and proud to call you my dad.
Here, deep inside my heart you'll always be.
I would give up everything I have just to hug you one
more time.
I remember the last time I held your hand and how you
looked at me in the eyes.
If only I could turn back the time I would have never let
you go.
I felt the world stop and my heart stop beating when they
told me you were gone.
How I wish I were only dreaming.
Just like the rain, tears fell down from my eyes; I couldn't
speak for a while.
Thank you, Dad,
For always understanding, listening, caring, and loving me
your whole life.
The greatest gift God gave me was YOU ... my dad.
It's difficult to let you go, but I must.
I must return the gift God gave me.

Lea Gomez

5 Years and 22 Days!

January 21, 2019

I realise now when talking to people they often think my dad passed last year or a few months ago, so when I say it was five years ago there is this noticeable silence, which I read as 'That long ago and you are still grieving??' Of course this could be my perception and not theirs.

  I have decided I don't want to ever get over my father's death. No, I am not wallowing nor am I stuck. I am fine and am not looking for sympathy either this is just an honest reflection. A lot of folk think after a few months or maybe a year or two we should have been healed. So, what does healing actually mean? Complete recovery and normality? Or does it mean you need to hide how you feel or, worse still, apologise for missing your loved one after five years?

  I remember on day thirteen I hit the grief rock. My heart was bleeding and there was this massive sense of incompleteness, a sort of haemorrhage where you literally think, I am not going to survive this heartbreak. After five years I still miss my dad. I drink freshly made juice and regret not making this often enough for my dad though we had the juicer back then. I find a new recipe and think, why did I not make this for Dad, he would have liked it too. I hear the birds singing and have this overwhelming desire to say, 'Dado, can you hear that?' I hear a song come on the radio and I want to hold his hand and dance but can't … I wake up in the middle of the night and think how he and I would have enjoyed a bowl of cornflakes at the crack of dawn … you know all those silly things, significant yet not so trivial things which matter to me. The shocking thing is these things still happen in my daily life. I guess it is the measure of the impact he had on my life.

It can feel raw. Surprisingly, I found the fifth death anniversary harder than the ones before. Christmas was equally harder this time, too. No, this is not a relapse of grief this is a realisation that he will always play a big part in my life. The fact is five years later, I can see clearly that my world had changed for good when he died; that there is still this massive hole which will always remain open. A big wide gaping hole which I know is there but others can't see.

Hardly a day goes by when I do not remember him. I hear some music which I think he would have liked or see the House of Commons debate and I think he would have had a witty observation about the Brexit deal and present state of affairs. Bottom line, my dad is there during my twenty-four hours, even at busy times, happy times and disappointing times. And you know what, I am happy he is in my thoughts and imagination.

They say we must live our lives so when we are no more we are missed. Well, my dad left a space that will never be filled. It is not a sad emptiness but a soft emptiness. It's as though he carefully chiselled the edges of that hole into my life. His place in my life is immeasurable and permanent.

Losing a father is not an injury from which you can be healed or a scar that will fade in time. His absence I shall feel forever which I consider to be a good thing.

Since my dad's death I have become aware of my own mortality, so much so that I pretty much do what pleases me. Sounds selfish but I would call it being true to me. Now I am relaxed about his physical death because I believe we are just a thought away from each other.

I will end my post on a positive note because I want those out there to know that you will do more than survive this maze of grief just as I did. This morning I did a podcast on grief and mental wellness. It helped because the interviewer made it effortless but I honestly don't think I would've been capable of doing it before now. If you are on this journey give yourself permission to grieve. Don't apologise for how you feel but embrace the hurting you. Be kind to you and honour this loss by living life on your terms.

> *'Tears water our growth.'*
> **(William Shakespeare)**

And I can't resist this quote by my favourite writer and poet, Maya Angelou: 'My mission in life is not merely to survive, but to thrive; and to do so with some passion, some compassion, some humour, and some style.'

Peace be with you.

DMP

The Impossible Void

March 3, 2019

It's been a while. I ask myself, it's five years now surely I'm over the worst part of my grief journey but then it hits me sideways. I lose my balance momentarily so I am forced to hit the pause button, I retreat, reflect and then get up to carry on to face another day. I move from being utterly grateful for all the blessings to feeling equally empty and lost.

To be honest I feel tired of trying to fill the void left by my dad, it's just not possible.

Since my father's death my life has been like a capsule of constant change. I started this journey with one aim, which was to survive. I keep saying to myself I have so much going on in my life and so many things to be very grateful for, yet deep down the one person whose approval and smile I crave for I cannot have. I remember writing in my post in the early days a quote which I read, which went along the lines of: 'grief will either break you or make you. It will smash you into pieces and if you make it through you will look the same but inside you will be bruised, battered, misshaped but even stronger'. The many stories I have read and the many quotes I have read on what it is like to walk through the jungle of grief now makes sense. The bottom line is that grief is so personal, as personal as our DNA. There is no best before date or end date, it just is. I am resigned to feeling this massive void in my being for the rest of my life no matter what I do and what I have.

Sometimes we question if our loved ones who've gone are with us. Last Saturday I had a surreal experience.

I was visiting the Mind Body Spirit Festival nearby; I'd gone there to support a friend. There I got talking to this guy who was a medium. Now until now I've not been tempted to see one because I've always felt a connection with my father. This chap said he had my father there and he had a message for me. The message was keep wearing his ring and that I'm on the right track. I remember very clearly I was feeling cold and my hands were in my pocket so I don't think he had the chance to see my hands.

I don't want to say I endorse seeing a medium. This was my first encounter and it was a chance meeting.

As it happens I am wearing my dad's ring which he had made for him when he was nineteen, it has his name engraved on it. My dad gifted his ring to me before he passed saying I was the only one who was entitled to it.

Since my father's death I've shed some tears. I have sobbed my heart out just twice and I know exactly when. What is hard to appreciate by those who've not experienced the loss of a loved one is that the pain of loss or separation is just as real, if not more so, than any imaginable physical pain. Yet we are so remarkably resilient that we can keep going, we can even smile and live a full life, which surely we must aim to do so for our sake and as a tribute to the soul we loved so much.

My father was an optimistic soul and he was never held back by anything.

I always like to end my post on a hopeful note. I will leave you with this beautiful quote by William Wordsworth:

'We will grieve not, rather find the strength in what remains behind.'

I'd add that what remains behind is us; you, me and this beautiful universe.

Peace be with you.

DMP

My Father's Legacy

April 1, 2019

It is five years, three months and two days since I became an orphan. Losing my dad has made me acutely aware that I am next in the queue. There is no pity or sadness just a recognition of the seismic emotional change and growth. My dad would say, finally I have grown up but I still have a lot to learn.

Death can be an invaluable friend if we see death in that light. Certainly my dad knew how to live in the NOW. His difficult days never held him back. He had this amazing innate ability to see the bigger picture and enjoy the present. My parents separated when I was five. My dad raised his children, ran his business and did what he believed he had to do for the greater cause of humanity. He never re-married, so as a single parent, which in those days was rare especially for a man, and without any family network to rely on, he got on with doing his duty towards his children and the community. I always admired him for the sacrifices he made.

Legacy can be a burden or a gift depending on our perspective.

Last week I had the good fortune of attending an 80th birthday party. Almost sixty years ago, this lady and two women, including my mother, travelled together on a steamer from India to England with their little children in tow.

She happens to be the only person there who knew both my parents quite well. Around 200 guests were invited at this very exclusive celebration.

She went on to acknowledge that my father was a pioneer because it was my father who founded the first Hindu temple in this country. Since then there are of course many more majestic Hindu temples all around the UK, but someone had to have a vision and someone had to make a start. In those days there was a small group of Hindu families but they had no community hub to get together. My dad was not a religious man but he was astute enough to know how the community could be brought together. He was blessed with some fine kindred spirits who helped him with this vision. My father wrote more than thirty handwritten letters to various estate agents in the city asking them to bear in mind the need for a large building with a decent amount of land around it. (In those days there was no email.) A building was bought from the Salvation Army and now that temple has been in place for more than fifty-two years. The temple started with a handful of people using their own homes as collateral to acquire this splendid property, which included my father.

   New visitors to the temple will not be privy to this but for me it is a matter of deep personal honour for my father to be recognised in this way. As my father was mentioned, I stood up to accept this accolade amidst a round of applause. My only qualification or entitlement to receive this gift was because I was there as his daughter. I remember feeling proud beyond words. It was wonderful to hear my father's contribution recognised in such a public way.

   Early this month there was another event; this was at the banqueting suite at our local Civic Hall. It was an event hosted to mark forty years of a local hospice. I had received bereavement counselling through this hospice so I do, when the opportunity arises, like to lend my support. I had been interviewed for the event at home. As this was being

shown on the big screen I was talking about the great work the hospice does for our city. In the backdrop my father's picture was on display then the Eureka moment happened … around thirty-five years ago in this very same banqueting suite at the Civic Hall my father had hosted a reception for the Indian High Commissioner. Amongst the dignitaries were Sir Keith Joseph, the then Education Secretary, and Sir Denis Healey, Deputy Leader of the Labour Party. I remember running down the steps to get their autographs. I thought, wow, here we are again the both of us after all those years, amazing grace. I'd forgotten about this event like I have so many such events but I am glad I made the connection. I came home with a big smile on my face feeling mighty proud. Now, my dad was not an educated man, nor was he part of an elite group but he had the uncanny ability to connect with many. I feel so happy just thinking about that.

I am his youngest and the luckiest of them all as I carry his legacy. It is a responsibility I am very aware of and I know that while I can never match him in the many things he did and the way he made people feel, I do aspire to be good enough so that when people look me they see a bit of my father in me.

To conclude, on the subject of death and legacy we are all our parents' legacy or gift to the world. We have a responsibility to add value for the next generation like they did with their pioneering hard work. Life was not easy for them. They did more than just provide for their families and we need to acknowledge their contribution and follow in their footsteps as well as leave our own mark in the sand. We must do so in our unique way, but no matter how important we believe ourselves to be we must never forget we are because of them. I am proud to be known as my father's daughter, I do not need any other accolades or labels.

I heard a lovely talk on the subject of death recently. The essence of it was that we must see death as a trusted adviser to remind us to be in the NOW, especially when we feel agitated or stressed by the most mundane of things. Life is happening when we are on our way busy going somewhere or doing something sometimes important and necessary, sometimes not. Now, if we think about this carefully, we would not have music but for the silence in between the notes yet we hardly notice the silence as we are too absorbed in the doing part.

My take from this experience is this. It helps to remember we have a limited life span. We only have one chance to live life and get it 'right'. It is inevitable that one day we too will die. What do we want our legacy to be? Hopefully, it is to make a difference and to leave a positive, albeit tiny, mark on the world.

Pause, especially when we feel we can't breathe. Listen to our inner voice that is our guide.

Say yes (within reason) to life, and finally, when possible rest and be kind to you because you matter. We all matter. We are one part of the whole. Enough said, you will understand.

Peace be with you.

DMP

101 Years and Not Out!

April 23, 2019

I celebrated my father's birthday on 21st April in a low-key manner but in a way I hope he would have approved. My father and I spent our last proper holiday together in Dubai with my nephew so I decided to celebrate this day in Dubai, which is where I write this. I still have to think slightly ahead when these special days are on the horizon so I have a degree of control, so this was something I had planned a while back. Right until I started packing, which was on the morning of my travel, I wasn't really in the mood for the holiday but was going through the motions in the hope that going away meant I would be away from the memories.

I arrived in Dubai on the morning of my father's birthday. I went to the beach, walked on the sand, looked up and said a little thank you to him for being with me. I enjoyed a cup of Yorkshire tea to recover from my journey and an excessively indulgent carrot cake to celebrate my dad's 101st birthday. Very low key compared with the past. I could not emulate what I did last year, which was the London Marathon, but this was quite fine too.

Later on I went to an Ashram in Dubai for a meditation session. So the birthday was over. Two days on (I think) I received a sign from my dad. One evening, sat in an Italian restaurant where the lighting was quite dim, I saw a couple on the opposite table sitting about fifteen feet away. The side profile of the gentleman was so much like my dad's and the mannerisms, the laughter, the gestures, gosh my heart sank. I thought, he looks just like my father, and it was surreal. I could feel my eyes filling up and thought this is not a place where you want to be misty eyed. I looked down to steady myself. I asked the girl who came to serve me if the couple spoke any English and she said a bit. I waited a while then got up and walked over to them. I told them he reminded me of my father. The gentleman up close was much younger than my dad but honestly the side profile had an uncanny resemblance. He was lovely and very understanding. I showed a picture of my father, both he and his wife agreed that there was some resemblance. We had a brief chat about our holidays; they were from Sweden on a flying visit, like me. We parted with a smile and a story connecting us.

This has never happened to me before, where I have seen someone and thought he looks like my dad. Why now and why here? I don't have the answer but I do believe there is a lot more I do not see or even understand.

As time goes by, I've noticed I think and see a younger version of my father even in my dreams so when I saw this chap he reminded me of how full of life my dad was when he was around ninety. In fact, my dad was in his late 80s when we travelled together to Egypt. It is a long story but my father and I cut our journey to Egypt short and almost ran free like two escapees from a group of much younger folk acting cautiously!

Oddly, just before this incident I had exchanged a message with my grand-nephew, Dishant, who is in Canada. We were exchanging details of the books we were reading. I told Dishant he may want to read Paulo Coelho's book, **The Alchemist**. In that book the author talks about how every single detail of our life is mapped out as though it is neatly designed to the most minute of details. A chance meeting is not really a coincidence. What the significance of this is I don't know, but I know this much, my father is still watching over me!

Happy birthday Dad. I love you.

Peace be with you.

DMP

5 Years, 5 Months and 18 Days...

June 17, 2019

Sometimes words are not important, it just is. Father's Day came and went, yet another day to feel the huge void and feel deeply grateful in equal measure. I shared the following thoughts with my close friends who, like me, are members of the fatherless club.

Thinking of you as we mark yet another Father's Day and feel the absence of our precious Dads.

But for us Father's Day is every day as our fathers are tucked away in our hearts.

We are blessed to have this beautiful connection with them. Enough said, you know.

Sending you much love.

Finding it hard to make sense of my emotions and to find the words that come close to what I feel, I searched and found this gem on the following page which I will share with you.

If you or someone close to you is feeling the ache of the loss of someone you loved dearly, please don't give up on them or on yourself. One step at a time ... they can hear you.

Wishing you much love and peace.

Peace be with you.

DMP

Happy Father's Day

I was not sure what to get you
On this very special day
So I decided to write this poem from my heart
I have some things I need to say:
I would first like to thank you,
For never giving up on me.
You pushed me when I needed it
And through your eyes I've learned to see
We cannot give up when times are tough
We've got to learn to lose before we can win
And if I shall ever fall
I know I will always get back up again
Thanks to you, I hold my head high
And carry myself with pride
Thanks to you, I am somebody
Who will never run and hide
Through you I've learned to face my fears
And take each day as it comes
You cannot take anything with you when you're gone
What's done is done
You lead by example
And because of you, I've learned a lot
Thanks to all the dedication that you have demonstrated
And the many many times that you have fought
You have fought for our existence
You have fought for everyone in your life
Never have I seen you give up
And thus in me you've instilled the fight
Never will I back down
For what I think is right
You've given me the will and determination

You've given me the might
To learn how to stand up
And learn to take a fall
But most of all, Dad
I've learned you will never stop loving me at all

Elisa Garcia

I Count My Blessings

June 30, 2019

I count my blessings…
 In this heat I sat outside and these words came to me…
 I count my blessings.
 Things turn out perfect. Just as they are meant to not a second sooner or later but with perfect precision.
 Every situation we face and every person we encounter is there for a reason. Happy situations and kind souls make our heart sing, whereas difficulties and challenging people are our teachers.
 There's a saying: 'God's delays are not God's denials'. Same way hardship is not a punishment, it's there to help us grow. God knows our true potential but do we?
 When we are tested it is to help us realise our true capabilities. Until we walk through the fire, metaphorically speaking, we don't sense how resilient, vulnerable yet strong we really are.
 A friend once said, 'A Samurai sword is tossed and turned a thousand times over in baking heat to make it tough, sharp and super flexible.' More elegantly put by him, 'tempered in the heat of the flame.'
 Now. Imagine.
 Just like a Samurai sword going through the heat and the baking process, our hardships and many heartaches have the power to transform us to be like a razor sharp sword, which, in the hands of a capable warrior, has the potential to cut through most of the challenges we face in our day-to-day lives.
 Now imagine our heart. The heart is like a sword. It's fragile

and it can break.

It hurts, it feels pain and often feels it is invisible to the owner of the heart and those around.

Now a warrior needs a strong yet versatile sword to make him invincible.

We can be focused and unfazed, the strength is within us but we are tested, often to the point of overwhelming despair by things outside our control. We don't know our own greatness.

The obstacles and challenges that push us to the limit are our blessings.

I came to the subject of counting my blessings when I was reflecting on the quality and depth of my relationship with my dad. I don't have the words to really explain what this means to me but it still amazes me how he knew what I was thinking well before I did. Often I didn't know what I was thinking but he did. I heard him before he said anything. I appreciate the connection with my father even more.

The power of unspoken communication. Effortless and priceless. The foundation of such a relationship is trust and unconditional love.

Amongst my blessings the relationship with my father is at the top of the tree.

Now, we are lucky if we have such a connection with one person, but very, very lucky if we come close to it with more than one person.

We often have some people in our lives with whom we have nothing in common. We probably wouldn't converse with them ever but for the 'must put up with them' talk in our head.

I'm blessed with this experience too, but I'm glad as they have taught me so much.

I'm glad I count this as one of my many blessings too.

As I count my blessings I think of my generous friends.

I have a handful of very close, soulful and loyal friends. They were there for me when I was crumbling or when I had doubts.

My friends are the ones who get me. They listen to me and they give me their attention without any reservation. They encourage me and believe in me when I doubt myself.

They don't want anything in return. They just want me to be happy. They really care and when they say, 'How are you?' they actually mean it. They clear their schedule to listen to me pour my heart out. I thank my close friends for being there for me.

So, as I count my blessings I think of you as you read this. I'm blessed and honoured to connect with you as well. Our paths have crossed for a reason. You encourage me to keep going.

I wish you well and hope you too, like a Samurai warrior, are able to recognise your own strength to help you through the challenges of life.

When I count my blessings I count YOU twice.

Peace be with you.

DMP

Grief – A Chance Of Discovery

August 4, 2019

Life is a journey, as is grief, and whilst we have breath if we embrace both we stand a chance of discovery. This is the conclusion I have come to after five years and seven months of walking, sometimes stumbling and sometimes running through the valley of grief.

Emotional intelligence is a gift as we often find a sense of disconnect when others fail to understand us because we have no words or ways to describe what we are going through, especially when we are struggling to fathom what is happening to us. My father was blessed with emotional intelligence in abundance. He could read me in an instant, whereas it has taken me some time to gain an insight into my own soul and this is just the beginning.

So, how about us trying to reconnect with our self. Over the past five years I have sensed my own death, in fact, often I felt I was living but a part of me had died when my father died. Looking back that sounds dramatic and even an extreme view but I do remember feeling I was utterly lost. My anchor and my rock disappeared, who am I and what is my calling now, these were the many questions I had. Then to top it off there was the physical separation, the absence of this huge figure in my life. As if he was taken away from me forever. Fortunately, the spiritual connection with my father has endured and, in fact, I feel even closer to him than I did in life.

I think life is a journey or to put it crudely a process. You wake up then you wake up some more then the self dies, and so the evolution of consciousness and discovery goes on. Sue Monk Kidd talks about how God created this world. Starting with a seed and a sprout and a flower before it goes back to being a seed.

Life and grief is a journey of unfolding and greater awareness. We become more aware of our inner strength and vulnerability. At the same time we grow a bit more compassionate, more loving and more appreciative of our existence and those around us. That is life in its magical lifelong spiralling form. Hopefully, it is going upwards in terms of awareness.

Taking this one step further, aren't we a miracle in motion? Motion is movement, we are not quite there yet but we are in motion, going through recovery and discovery. If we can manage to experience both recovery and discovery at the same time then there is hope that we can embrace the loss of a loved one as an enlightening exponential experience. During this journey we die many times and then learn to live again but this time with a greater sense of appreciation and clarity.

I started this post talking about my walking, stumbling and running through the valley of grief. Those who know me well will understand the metaphors used here. I have experienced the lows and highs of what it is like to live without the presence of the most important person in my life, my father. It has not been easy but it certainly has been a journey of recovery and discovery of the self. I conclude with one message from my experience which may offer some hope to those on a similar journey and it is this.

Life is a journey and whilst we have breath it is far better to experience each breath as if it is our last and live life to the full. Grief is part of life. Some of us will never, not feel the sadness or emptiness left in our hearts by the death of a very significant person in our lives. They left leaving us with a beautiful big gaping hole which they carefully chiselled like a Michelangelo sculpture in our hearts. If you could touch the edges of this hole you will feel the ruggedness of each single memory and emotion imprinted with love.

We were the chosen ones to have been granted this loving being in our life. Their 'temporary' absence is bound to feel like a massive crash but the fact that you have experienced this is a testament to you. You are a miracle, a miracle in motion on the path of recovery and discovery of your truest self.

Peace be with you.

DMP

One Wish...

September 7, 2019

I cannot believe that the one person in the world I want to read this post, never actually will. My father was my everything. Words simply cannot and will not ever do justice to what this amazing, kind, wonderful, beautiful, generous, loving and caring man meant to me and the people around him.

Words cannot and will not ever truly describe, even with my ability to express, the gaping hole in my world now since his passing. It has been five years, eight months and eight days to the day as I write this since he left, and it feels like yesterday.

Every now and then the universe produces a very special kind of soul. He was that to me. I had the good fortune of having him as my father. We were inseparable yet different. I still cannot bring myself to delete my dad's numbers from my mobile phone, and when I look at his picture though I smile there is heartache. Sometimes, without any reason, tears overflow and I realise though I have come a long way there is a yearning to sit next to him one last time and laugh out loud again. One wish that cannot happen in this lifetime. I write this because I would never have achieved anything without my father. If I have helped anyone in anyway or inspired anyone, it is all down to my remarkable and extraordinary father. Put simply, I am because of him.

Two weeks ago I had a bench placed at our local park where Dad and I used to go for long walks. It is a strong and well-made bench made of teak and the plaque reads:

What a wonderful world
Sit down and enjoy the view
In loving memory of Manhar Patel
An Inspiration

My dad loved the song 'What a Wonderful World' by Louis Armstrong. This park is a gift to our community and is a really special place of natural beauty. The bench is in a cosy and quiet spot surrounded by beautiful trees and on a clear day you can see the lake. When I heard the bench was in situ I went to see it as it was something I had wanted to do for a long time. Sitting on the bench, and around was a family having a picnic, I thought 'perfect'.

Sometimes I stop, turn off my mobile and just watch the beautiful tall trees swaying in the wind and the clear sky. I remember the poem 'Footsteps in the Sand' written in 1936 by Mary Stevenson, there's a line in there: 'Lord, you said once, you'd walk with me all the way, but I noticed that during my saddest and most troublesome times of my life, there was only one set of footprints. I don't understand why, when I needed you the most, you would leave me. He replied, "When you say only one set of footprints, it was then I carried you."'

I have seen God through my father's loving eyes. There have been many moments since my father's passing when I have needed him the most and I quite possibly didn't realise then but he was there.

Faith and love are two powerful parts of our life. Sometimes we just have to believe we will make it to the next day. Just don't give up hoping that you will make it through because you will.

Peace be with you.

DMP

Love Letter to My Father

October 27, 2019

Dear Dado,

Hi, hello and namaste Pops. How are you doing? I bet you're marking Diwali in your flamboyant style. Everyone is running around you looking after your many friends and guests and you are holding court charming everyone with your brilliant conversations.

Dado today is Diwali, yes, my sixth Diwali (the festival of light) without your physical presence but I feel closer to you now than we were in life. Strange isn't it! It is 2,127 days to be precise.

Yesterday, while talking to a friend, I realised again that I will never ever feel the closeness of heart that I have with you with anyone else, never. It won't ever happen. We were two peas in a pod, father and daughter. Kindred spirits and soulmates. I thank God for the gift of you in my life. The love I have from you will help me through until the end of my days. It is enough and I can't ask for more from God. He has given me the ultimate gift of unconditional love from my father.

I remember our last Diwali together here in 2013. As usual I cooked a lot of your favourite sweets and together we celebrated the festival of lights in our own big way. Our home was open to friends and as usual I was running around spinning plates, yet feeling happy because it was joyful to see everyone here who had come to see you. My first Diwali after you passed I remember not even lighting the candles and just working long hours trying to ignore

Diwali. It was too painful. When anyone asked where I was and what I was doing, you know by those kind souls inviting me over to join them, I wouldn't answer the phone. I just couldn't. My world was dark and hopeless then, I couldn't see beyond my grief and broken heart. I felt like a vase broken into a million pieces with absolutely no hope of being put back together. I feel so sad when I think of how bereft I was. Only difference now is that I am grateful for going through this journey of discovery.

In the early days I read a piece in ***The Spectator*** by Matthew Parris who wrote about never wanting to get over his father's death. I thought wow, here's somebody who understands. That's how I felt and still do. Why should I? I am my father's daughter, that is sacred and carries significance to me and who I am. The choice was clear even in the depth of despair: sink or swim. Being your daughter there was only one way to go.

Recently, I found myself comforting another bereaved orphan and found myself reflecting on how I coped. Walking for hours on end in the pouring rain with no destination in mind. My home is you. Sometimes I used to sit on the bench we used to sit on in our local park for hours on end crying my eyes out and feeling, God how do I go on and why. Will I ever find a reason to smile? I felt numb and sensitive to anything that reminded me of how colourful life could be. I couldn't even bring myself to paint my nails; there was nothing or nobody that gave me a reason to keep going. I was praying to God to take me to my dad.

Fast forward, here I am. I've never felt more close to you than now. There is not a day that goes by when I don't think of you or talk to you. Not a day goes by when I don't tell you about my day, my worries or my joyful moments. You are with me always and like the ray of sun I feel your warmth and I see your smiling eyes. You made me and I have your DNA how can we be separate? In my highs and lows, like before, you are still with me sharing my every moment. I never say 'my home' because it still is 'our home'. In every room there are reminders of you. I have learnt to live and I am grateful for our time together.

In life you brought out the best in me and in death you do much more. You've helped me find me.

I know no one will ever understand my inner workings like you. I didn't realise how lucky and blessed I was having you in my life when you were alive. I took you for granted and often argued with you I am sorry for hurting your feelings as I know I did many a time. I have had to examine every aspect of my existence and it has been painful. I have had to dig deep and sometimes I felt I needed you so badly I needed to put my head on your shoulder and cry my heart out but I managed to reconfigure our 'new' relationship and found comfort in carrying on as if my dad is still with me because you are. Ironic, the one person I needed when I was at my lowest because of you was YOU.

It is said that after death the soul either attains salvation or takes another birth. I am no expert in these matters but for me your soul and mine is an infinite energy and you and I are always connected regardless of which planet you and I are on.

So Dado, on this sixth Diwali as usual when I woke up and opened my eyes I said, 'Happy Diwali Dado' to you first. Tomorrow I will take your blessings on New Year's Day as I have always done. Nothing has changed.

Your daughter is strong and is still walking like you. I won't give up until I have completed my Dharma on earth. Last Sunday, Pops, I ran my second marathon, yes who would have thought I was capable of running 10k, let alone two marathons? As I came to the finishing line I could see you standing there with open arms smiling with pride saying, 'There's my daughter.' The place where I ran the marathon, six years ago in October, is where I returned to the world of law eight months after your passing to work as a locum solicitor. The route of the marathon took me over a bridge I had walked over many a time six years back. Then I was looking for ways to end my life, now that thought never enters my head. What's happened in between? I had to grow up. I had to dig really deep to climb out of a hole. You helped me, Dad, through my darkest hour. You were there for me as you are now. As I came through the finishing line I was cheered on by my wonderful coach who saw the running potential in me when I could see no hope. You sent so many angels to help me through this agonising yet enlightening journey and I am grateful to each one of them. You sent them for me, thank you.

  The marathon route included some long and quiet country lanes and by about seventeen miles it rained heavily. I found myself running alone surrounded by awesome trees in the beautiful countryside with the occasional sighting of some cows and marshals. I was wet through and even your handkerchief, which I always take on my runs, was soaking wet, the thought of giving up at twenty miles never occurred to me though. The next day a friend asked me what kept me going in those quiet and challenging moments as there were moments when I wanted to lie down on the road as the legs were so tired. I replied to my friend after pausing for a moment and said, 'I was running with the Lord on my right and Dad on my left.' I wasn't running alone there were hidden forces willing me on, how else would I have completed the run plus beat my personal best by fifty-seven minutes!! You know, Dad, just before this run

I felt unprepared; I thought I hadn't trained enough but I was wrong, I was ready. On the morning of my run a friend texted me to say many people believe in me. He was right – all those people with you have helped me through.

My running is a living metaphor of my journey of the past six years. I know I will keep going. I still don't know where exactly but I know I'm coming home to you. Entering a marathon is quite an audacious act, let alone run it and complete it. I have the audacity to say I am still standing with the Lord and my dad by my side.

I am slowly getting to a point of equilibrium. Your death never made us apart and we can never be apart. Like the morning sun which comes out no matter what, you, my father, are always with me every step of the way. I hear you and feel you in every cell of my being.

Thank you for being my ineffable father.

Happy Diwali my brilliant father, I love you Dado and always will. Any doubt? I hope not.

Your grateful daughter,

Daxa
Diwali, Year 2076.

Almost 6 Years

November 20, 2019

'We shall not cease from exploration, and the end of all our exploring will be to arrive where we started and know the place for the first time.'
(T.S. Eliot)

I love this quote as it reminds me that we are constantly seeking the truth, yet when we feel we have the answers we start all over again from the beginning. This coming December, on the 30th, it will be six years since my wonderful father passed away. Six years, which is only seventy-two months, seems a long time, almost an eternity, yet it feels like only yesterday he and I were seated at the dining table having tea together. My life was on a linear path until then, before it was disrupted big style. The world goes on regardless but for those of us who have lost someone we love the most it's as though we go from grinding to a complete halt to eventually learning to adjust to what is. I live with a massive hole in my being and it is still the same size. A void. Knowing that I will never hear him say, 'I am proud of you' but knowing also that he is.

As I write this I do so from a retreat I visited a year before my father passed, for some respite. The year after he passed I came back again to make sense of my aching heart. I recall sitting on a bench by the river and pouring my heart out to a stranger who was kind enough to listen. The bench is surrounded by some very mature trees where you can see the roots all spread out. I remember also then hugging a tree. In search of answers as to what my relationship now was with my late father I met with some spiritual leaders, one of whom told me that my father on his death disconnected all his connections with me. Of course that just wasn't what I wanted to hear, plus it gave me no comfort at all. Then I met another who simply said, 'When you feel you are at sea with your emotions just sit in front of your father's picture, look into his eyes and sit in silence, you will in time learn to keep going.' That was a palatable gem of advice which I did follow. Today, I sat on that same bench with mixed feelings of calmness and numbness as I reflected on my journey. I touched the same tree (I didn't hug it) hoping that it would take me a little closer to the same feeling I used to get when I touched my father's hands. This tree is old, tall and solid. It stands majestically still. I thought maybe this is as close as it gets to being physically closer to my dad. Perhaps it is and perhaps that's as good as it gets, until one day I hope I am with him where once again my dad and I will sit down at the dining table and enjoy a cup of tea and chat.

Coming here is a pilgrimage of sorts. I met some people here who have seen me on and off during the last six years. They won't know but they too played a part in my healing. When I travel to work I see this sign in neon lights: 'EVERYTHING IS CONNECTED'. I also see the words on a wall: 'Don't break your tender heart' but I'd rather say, 'TAKE CARE OF YOUR TENDER HEART'. I do believe everything is connected with precision and the right people come into our lives just at the right time to help us. This makes sense when we look back and see how far we have travelled and how we have been helped in the most unexpected ways. Even my coming here just before the sixth anniversary is for a reason, as it is a vital reminder that I am still climbing my Mt. Everest. Maybe I am at base camp but that's fine too, I know I will make it to the summit one day and when I do I will see my father's smiling face and loving eyes. He

will tell me again how proud he is of me. Sometimes, I think when God gave us a father he did so to remind us of what God is like: kind, loving and generous to a fault. There is no substitute for the unconditional love of a father.

If I were to offer some hope to another on a similar journey it is this. This is your earthquake. Hit the emergency brakes and go slow. It is painful and you have a right to be in survival mode. Slowly but surely you will find a way to keep going and you will; if I can make it to this point so can you.

Be kind to you.

Peace be with you.

DMP

6 Years and 6 Weeks!

February 20, 2020

This is supposed to get easy and yes, I am supposed to get better at this but it doesn't always work like that. I have been quiet of late as during December I struggled with yet another Christmas without my dad and yet another anniversary. I almost forgot that I can slide back and feel sad. The combination of the festive season, the anniversary and the arrival of the New Year has made December my dreaded month, so I kind of gave in. I retreated and felt sorry for myself. With January came the sixth anniversary of the funeral. I remember I was working from home on my laptop and out of nowhere tears came streaming down my face. I wondered if anyone else actually knew what date it was then I thought what an unreasonable expectation on my part. I lived with him and I lived his death. He is my father and my father only.

> *'Sometimes the finest command of language is to say nothing.'*
> **(David Baird)**

Sometimes words don't do justice. During December I decided to read a book I had read soon after my father's passing to see how far I had come and how I felt. I read ***A Grief Observed*** by C.S. Lewis. His writing captured my heart and I finished the book in one sitting. My conclusion was that his words and sentiments still resonated but I had become a bit more pragmatic. I felt a sense of humility that like so many out there who have had to endure the loss of a very important person in their lives, I too had gone through the 'fire' and I understand. C.S. Lewis talks of how he questioned everything, including the presence of God.

Hilary Mantel describes his book very eloquently, she says, 'Lewis's book is a lucid description of an obscure, muddled process, a process almost universal, one with no logic and no timetable'. That says it all. A deeply enlightening yet painful experience with no logic or time frame is a good description of grief.

My father's role in my life is so huge that the void is equally massive hence the retreat to make sense. I am of course glad that he is not in physical distress but the hole in my being is my sense of belonging, my home. Where he was I belonged, now I am drifting with no anchor and no shore to reach. I don't know if all orphan adults relate to this but I remember once my dad said after his eighty-six-year-old mother passed that even though he had his family and me, the one person whom he would go home to was his mother. Without her he felt adrift. I understand that sentiment now.

It is a strange existence on the one hand, one keeps going to do what one must and, as they say life, goes on regardless. On the other hand, our lives come to an abrupt halt and, in fact, our lives are changed forever, only we don't get to comprehend how much until months and years after. The other day I went for a long run and ran past our old home. I looked up where to my bedroom used to be and remembered how my dad had given each room a name. We had the blue room, the pink room and so on. I smiled thinking how meticulous he was; even his methodical filing system was second to none. There is even a sling in the filing cabinet with a label 'Sweet and sour'! I have not altered the filing system and I have found myself doing the same thing he used to do but I didn't then take much notice, or so I thought. Instead of using Post-it Notes® he would always use the back of used paper by carefully cutting it with a ruler so that each piece of paper was the exact size. This would be our stash of scrap paper to write the shopping list or list of jobs to do. I do it exactly how he used to do, I mean I cannot even bring myself to open a letter without using a letter opener or draw a line without using a ruler, all things I unconsciously picked up from him.

He was ahead of his time back in the days when we didn't talk so much about the environment. I remember he wrote on the white board 'BUY LESS, USE LESS AND RECYCLE'. I also remember with a degree of pride how my father got a big picture of Nelson Mandela, which he prominently placed on the back wall of our shop, this was well before Nelson Mandela's release from prison in 1990. I can still see the words on the picture, it read: 'Free Madiba'. Many of our customers thought we were from South Africa, which was funny as we have no connections there. He was a man with a strong sense of civic duty and a citizen of the world.

Thinking of my dad I feel immensely proud and blessed that I had the chance to spend time with this great man whom I call my father. What he meant to me only I will know and I am sure you must feel the same about your loved one. We share, through the medium of this blog, a synergy of hope and understanding of what is after all a universal experience. Love and loss are two sides of the coin, we can't have one without the other, yet I am sure you too wouldn't want it any other way.

Peace be with you.

DMP

And finally, what I meant to say....

June 21, 2020 (Father's Day)

Dear Dado

What I meant to say was... How can I possibly say goodbye to the person who was the first to hold me, the first to feed me, and the first to make me feel loved?

From a distance I watched you move about doing the mundane tasks that to everyone else seems so routine. But for me, the tasks you lovingly completed year after year built and reinforced the foundation, the structure that made my world a safe and comfortable place to grow.

All that I am and all that I have can be traced back to you. Whatever accomplishments I have made along the way would not have occurred without first believing in myself. And you, you were the person who always believed in me.

I am amazed at the number of times I hear your own words flow from my mouth. It warms me as I've come to understand that there is a part of you that will live on in me forever.

I pray that you will reach across from the other side to again touch my face and whisper in my ear.

For your warm and gentle presence in my life... for this, I will always be most thankful.

Yes, father, you inspire me!

Your grateful daughter,

DMP.

Adapted from a book by Michael E Murphy (2004) called "What I meant to say"

About the author

Daxa Patel, LLB (Hons), MBA, is a Resilience and Empowerment Coach dedicated to transforming adversity into empowerment and purpose. After stepping back from her successful career as a healthcare litigation solicitor and law firm partner, Daxa embraced her calling to guide others through life's challenges. Her journey of caring for her beloved father and navigating profound grief inspired her to share her story through writing. "My Dad and Me: A Journey of Love, Loss, and Life" is a heartfelt reflection on resilience and healing, drawn from her personal blogs.

Beyond her coaching practice, Daxa is a passionate advocate for marginalised voices, writing a weekly column for the Yorkshire Post. Her insights and experiences empower readers to embrace their potential and live authentically.

An accomplished marathon runner, Daxa completed the London Marathon in honour of her father's 100th birthday, embodying the spirit of perseverance and dedication. Daxa resides in Leeds, West Yorkshire, UK, where she continues to inspire and uplift through her work and writing. She shares her life with Oscar, her incredible German Shepherd, who carries on the legacy of her father's love for the breed.

Connect with Daxa:
www.daxapatelresilience.com
https://grievingmypapa.wordpress.com

- Writer, Author, Columnist, Resilience & Empowerment Coach, Entrepreneur.
- The Resilience Architect – Transforming Adversity into Empowerment and Purpose.

www.ingramcontent.com/pod-product-compliance
Lightning Source LLC
Chambersburg PA
CBHW040639100526
44585CB00039B/2824